Peter Poyntz Wright, who is married and lives in Somerset, holds a Masters Degree in architecture and is the author of three previous books. After eighteen years in industry he taught history at Huish Episcopi School, Langport, for nineteen years before retiring. His expertise is in the medieval and includes sixteen seasons' excavation at Glastonbury Abbey. He lectures widely on architectural topics and conducts tours to medieval sites at home and abroad. He has spent eight years investigating the Norman Conquest of England prior to writing this book.

Hastings

PETER POYNTZ WRIGHT

PHOENIX

A Windrush Press Book

A PHOENIX PAPERBACK

First published in Great Britain in 1996
by The Windrush Press
This paperback edition published in 2005
in association with The Windrush Press
by Phoenix,
an imprint of Orion Books Ltd,
Orion House, 5 Upper St Martin's Lane,
London WC2H 9EA

The Windrush Press
Windrush House
12 Adlestrop
Moreton-in-Marsh
Glos GL56 0YN

Phoenix Paperbacks
Sterling Publishing Co Inc
387 Park Avenue South
New York
NY 10016-8810
USA

1 3 5 7 9 10 8 6 4 2

Copyright © Peter Poyntz Wright 1996, 1997, 1998

The right of Peter Poyntz Wright to be identified as the author of
this work has been asserted by him in accordance with the
Copyright, Designs and Patents Act 1988.

Parts of this book originally appeared in Peter Poyntz Wright's previous
book *The Battle of Hastings* published by Michael Russell (Publishing) Ltd
in 1986, which is now out of print.

A CIP catalogue record for this book
is available from the British Library.

ISBN 0 75381 994 5

Typeset at The Spartan Press Ltd,
Lymington, Hants

Printed and bound in Great Britain by
Clays Ltd, St Ives plc

www.orionbooks.co.uk

CONTENTS

LIST OF ILLUSTRATIONS

BLACK AND WHITE ILLUSTRATIONS SECTION

AUTHOR'S ACKNOWLEDGEMENTS
AND NOTE OF SOURCES

In the research for this book I have received help from many friends and colleagues; especially I wish to thank B. H. Rushton, B.Sc., Pauline Clarke, M.A., and Pam Burrough for their help in the research and presentation of the text, and to my sons Alexander and Oliver for their practical assistance. Finally I like to express my appreciation to my wife Gabrielle for her unfailing support and encouragement.

THE SOURCES

Much documentary material has survived from the century following the Battle of Hastings, and much research has been carried out over the last hundred years. What happened in the course of the battle is now fairly well understood, though it is still possible to interpret in more ways than one the events leading up to it. The purpose of this book is to bring together much evidence at present scattered and not easily accessible to the general reader together with a full background to the events leading up to 1066. The characters and lives of the two combatants are analysed in detail.

Most of the evidence expresses the Norman point of view. Hastings is unusual in having an almost contemporary pictorial account surviving in the Bayeux Tapestry; which is reliable on detail in spite of a strong political slant. Of the writers, the most prolific, and probably the most biased, was William of Poitiers, who wrote a biography of Duke William entitled *Gesta Guillelmi Ducis Normannorum*, probably between 1073 and 1074. William of

Poitiers was a Norman, born about the year 1020; in his youth he fought under Duke William of Normandy before studying and taking holy orders at Poitiers. After this he returned to the Duke as his chaplain, and finally became Archdeacon of Lisieux. His work, like the Tapestry, provides reliable knowledge on points of detail but he was William's man and expressed William's views.

William of Jumièges, another historian of the time, was a monk of the Abbey of Jumièges who wrote a personal history entitled *Gesta Normannorum Ducis* between 1070 and 1072. This gives a slightly different account of events but still from a Norman point of view. Guy, Bishop of Amiens, provides yet more details in *Carmen de Hastingae Proelio*, now generally accepted both as being his work and as having been completed by 1070, though this is challenged by Professor R. H. C. Davis who maintains it is a literary exercise of the second quarter of the twelfth century.

Later works completed within a century of the battle include the *Ecclesiastical History of England and Normandy*, written between 1123 and 1141 by Ordericus Vitalis, a monk and historian of St Evroul, and the *Roman de Rou* written in verse chronicles between 1160 and 1174 by a poet named Robert Wace, who was later made a canon of Bayeux Cathedral by Henry II.

The Saxon side of the story is provided by the *Anglo-Saxon Chronicle*, by William of Malmesbury, a monk and historian who wrote among other things *Gesta Regum Anglorum* and died c. 1142, and finally by Florence of Worcester, a monk and historian who wrote *Chronicon ex Chronicis* and died in 1118. His work was completed by John of Worcester by 1141.

Of the more recent research perhaps the greatest contribution has been made by Professor D. C. Douglas, though very substantial work was done by Professor E. A. Freeman and Sir Frank Stenton, and in connection with the Bayeux Tapestry by N. P. Brooks and H. E. Walker. Much further research and many smaller contributions have been made by numerous others.

The Events before the Battle

The battle that took place on the Senlac Ridge a few miles from Hastings on Saturday 14 October 1066 was the direct consequence of Edward the Confessor's dying without issue, and the indirect consequence of an 'oath' taken by Harold Godwinson of Wessex in 1064, pledging his support for William of Normandy's claim to the throne of England. This battle, the date of which is still etched on our consciousness, was paramount in the making of England as we know it. It was a battle fought on a knife edge throughout the day and it is questionable whether the best man won.

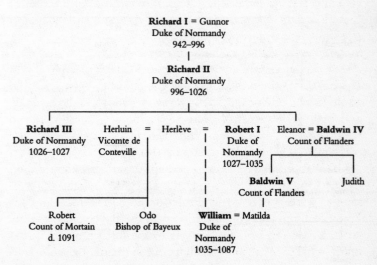

The Family of William, Duke of Normandy

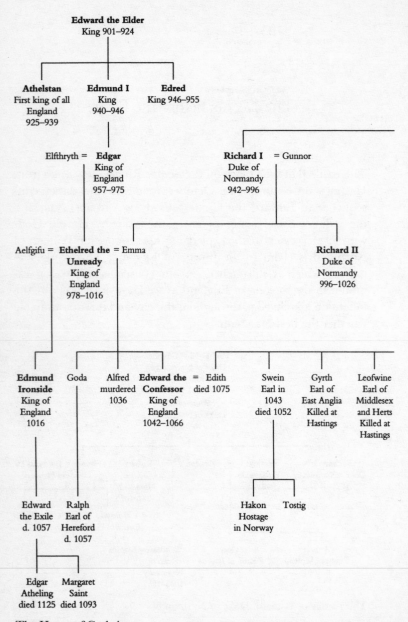

The House of Godwine

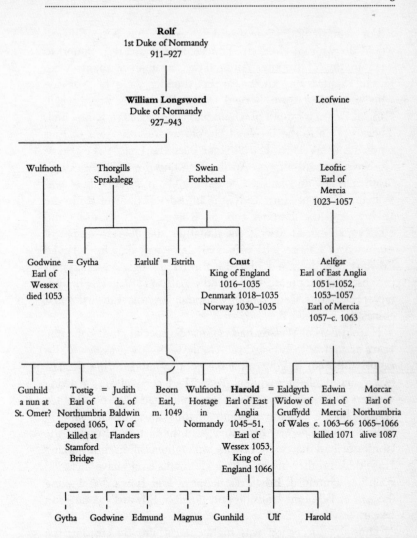

For years it had seemed almost certain that King Edward would die without children. The succession was thus bound to be a matter of dispute. Among the possible claimants were Harald Sigurdsson, known as Hardraade, King of Norway, who was feared from Bergen to the Black Sea, and Sweyn, King of Denmark, both of whom had claim through King Cnut. There were also the brothers Harold and Tostig, sons of Earl Godwine of Wessex. Harold had been Earl of Wessex since Godwine's death on 15 April 1053, and he was the king's brother-in-law and had no hereditary claim. Finally there was William, Duke of Normandy, the fifth descendant of Rollo the Viking and the bastard son of Robert of Normandy and Herlève, known as Arlette, the daughter of Fulbert, a tanner of the town of Falaise. His principal claim was that he believed Edward had promised him the throne in 1051, and that this promise was supported by Harold's 'oath' in 1064. His hereditary pretensions were tenuous, though he was Edward's first cousin once removed.

Harold Earl of Wessex had claims of a special kind. For some years he had been Edward the Confessor's closest associate, his right-hand man in governing the country, and during the last two years of his life, while Edward had been ill and growing weaker, in practice very nearly king. This had been possible for Harold because of the strength of the House of Godwine of Wessex, established by his father, and the fact that Edward the Confessor had married Godwine's daughter Edith, thus making Harold his brother-in-law. Other claimants could have included Ralph of Hereford, Edward's nephew, and Edward Aetheling the son of Edmund Ironside and possibly Edward's young son Edgar.

Thus the succession was highly uncertain. By custom, the Witan Gemoot, the Council of Wise Men, elected the king and an archbishop crowned him. It was on this principle that they acted when Edward died.

There seems little doubt that on his deathbed Edward indicated that he wished Harold to succeed him. Harold was at hand and was known to be capable of governing. Edward's choice was confirmed immediately after his death by the assembled Witan and Harold was crowned by Archbishop Aldred of York in Westminster Abbey on the Feast of the Epiphany, 6 January 1066, the same day that Edward was buried. He was the only commoner to acquire the crown of all England and the only king ever to die in the defence of his realm against a foreign invader.

Harold was born the second son of Earl Godwine of Wessex and his wife Gytha. Earl Godwine was the son of Wulfnoth and Gytha the daughter of Thorgills, both of Viking stock. He had five brothers, Swein, Tostig, Wulfnoth, Gyrth and Leofwine, and two sisters, Gunhild and Edith. He had two uncles, Earl Ulf, who was his mother's brother, and Aelfwig, who was Godwine's brother and became an abbot in 1063. Earl Beorn, Osbeorn and Swein Estrithson, King of Denmark who were Ulf's sons were his first cousins.

Born in 1022 during the reign of Cnut, Harold grew up at a time when his father was gaining confidence and influence as an earl, and was already twenty-two when Godwine assisted Edward the Confessor to the throne in 1042.

Created Earl of Wessex in 1018 by King Cnut Godwine clearly trained his sons in the arts of authority, management and administration as all but Wulfnoth made the rank of earl, Harold being appointed to East Anglia in 1045.

Harold did not marry at this stage but established a deep and long-lasting relationship with Edith Swannehals (Swan-neck) which survived until his death, and it seems likely that she bore him five of his seven children. Although this association was not sanctified by marriage it was acceptable within the social framework of the time.[1] The names of these five were Gytha, Godwine, Edmund, Magnus and Gunhild.

As the power and influence of the House of Godwine grew under the direction of Earl Godwine himself, Edward the Confessor became increasingly alarmed about the safety of his own position. Although he had been assisted to the throne by Earl

Godwine in 1042 and had created Swein an earl in 1043, and Harold one in 1045, he was becoming less sure of their loyalty, possibly because of his time spent in Normandy and the strong Norman background this gave him. In order to allay his fears Edward married Harold's sister Edith thus tying the Godwines with the English Royal House and making a challenge to the crown less likely.

Following this example very closely Harold married Ealdgyth shortly after he became king early in 1066. Ealdgyth was the sister of the brothers Edwin and Morcar and Earls of Mercia and Northumbria. They were of the House of Leofric and controlled much of the North of England, and although Harold had assisted in Morcar's appointment by Edward the Confessor he still felt it necessary to cement the association of the Houses of Godwine and Leofric after some difficulty in being accepted as King in the North.

Ealdgyth was the daughter of Aelfgar, Earl of Mercia, from 1057 to 1063, and the granddaughter of Leofric and Lady Godiva and apparently had inherited her grandmother's beauty. She had been married to Gruffydd of Wales, against whom Harold battled in his two Welsh campaigns, and who was killed by his own men in 1063. Harold carried his head to Edward the Confessor together with the prow of his ship. Ealdgyth was the mother of two of Harold's sons, Ulf and Harold, and as Harold himself was only married for a maximum of ten months these brothers were probably born posthumously and in any event must have been twins. Had the matter of the English succession after the Battle of Hastings been different, either of these twins would have been eminently suitable to take over the crown, and even the claim of the illegitimate children of Harold and Edith Swannehals would have stood up well against William who was also illegitimate.

That Harold was a great man is not really open to question. All the contemporary accounts of the time, with the exception of the panygerists of the Norman cause, refer to his many qualities of character and leadership. He was clearly a man of excellent physique, being strong fit and good-looking.[2] His powers of leadership and endurance are manifest by his Welsh campaigns and the amazing forced marches to and from the exhausting battle at Stamford Bridge. His ability to motivate and lead his men to such remarkable feats displays outstanding skill. His personal strength is illustrated in the Bayeux Tapestry where, on his campaigns with William, Harold is shown rescuing two Norman knights from the River Cousenon. He is carrying one on his shoulder and pulling the second out by hand. For these attributes Harold seems to have been well respected by friend and foe alike.

The only record of weakness in Harold, if that is what it was, is an account of an ailment immediately following his last Welsh campaign, from which he returned with partial paralysis. How extensive it was is not clear but was sufficient for Harold to pray before the Holy Rood at his foundation at Waltham Abbey[3] following which he became better.

In his dealings with others he is recorded as being wise, honest, frank and loyal. Over those whom he had authority he was merciful showing a good knowledge of Saxon law. To those over whom he was victorious in battle he displayed magnanimity and wisdom in settlement. However, he was always anxious to avoid military conflict, a characteristic he may have gained from Edward the Confessor, and his qualities as a conciliator were one of his greatest attributes.

Harold's strength lay in his wisdom and his ability to be both fair and firm and although some of his measures may seem cruel by present standards they were both accepted and respected by the standards of his time.

Although descended from Viking stock Harold regarded himself as a Saxon, or perhaps more accurately as an Englishman, and he was strongly patriotic. He had little time for insurrection from within and was angered by the military incursions of the Welsh. His aim was peace and prosperity under a firm and efficient government. His patriotism and his sense of justice brought about his dislike and mistrust of the Norman feudal system which he saw as cruel and divisive. When Harold finally faced William at Hastings he was genuinely fighting for the freedom of England from Norman suppression rather than defending his own crown. His attitude to the Normans did not stem from blind intolerance but a thorough knowledge of the Norman system and its language,[4] gained from his visits to Normandy, his association with Edward the Confessor whose formative years were spent in Normandy, and finally from his dealings with the many Normans who attended Edward's Court. During his visit to Normandy in 1064 Harold gained first-hand experience of the Normans' method of warfare and the cruelty they meted out to the vanquished. It was clear to Harold that the Saxon way of life and system of government were as good as, if not infinitely better, than that of the Normans, and it was the way of life in England that he was dedicated to defend.

By the Norman writers of the time Harold was maligned at every turn, being falsely accused of many crimes, and mis-represented in his policies and his decisions. Writing after Hastings William of Poitiers refers to him as 'stained with vice, a cruel murderer, purse-proud and puffed up with the profits of pillage'.[5] This was prompted by a desire to present Harold in the worst possible light for posterity, as the Normans felt that Harold had usurped the crown that was William's. Although much of this was conceived and written after the events, Harold must have been aware of the venomous feelings the Normans held for him during his short reign. These feelings were carefully nur-tured and publicised by William so that, as well as contriving to turn his invasion into a crusade, he made it a fulfilment of his personal vendetta against Harold.

It was Harold's courage that enabled him to overcome the political intrigues of his time, and his administrative ability both before and after Edward's death that allowed him to maintain the respect and loyalty of his subjects. No better is this illustrated than by the support he raised to defeat the invasion from the North at Stamford Bridge, and the support that almost defeated William at Hastings.

The one blemish on the otherwise upstanding character of Harold was his unprovoked attack on the men of Devon and Somerset near Porlock during his bid to return from banishment in 1052. Quite what the reasons were that motivated Harold to behave in this unusual way will probably never be clear. He must have been aware that England had been ruled for a year by Norman executives working under Edward, and it is possible that he saw the West Country folk as collaborators. Short of this or similar reasons it can only be construed that Harold wished to make a very strong mark to the effect that the Godwines were returning. His actions on this occasion must have been regretted by Harold for the rest of his life. Harold's relationship with Edward the Confessor was, apart from what must be considered a misunderstanding in 1051, a strong, loyal and long-lasting one. It sprang from the support that Edward received from Harold's father, and was greatly strengthened when Edward, worried by the rise in the power of the House of Godwine, married Harold's sister Edith on 23 January 1045,[6] when Harold was twenty-three.

Following the restoration of the Godwines in 1052, and after the death of Earl Godwine in 1053, the relationship between Edward and Harold became much closer. In assisting Edward in his royal duties Harold became as much involved with the running of the country as with his earldom of Wessex. Harold's ability to speak Norman-French meant that it was easy for Harold to communicate with Edward's many Norman friends and advisers, and as Edward still had many Norman leanings this may have helped to cement their personal relationship.

For ten years after his father's death Harold gained both regal experience and confidence, and after 1063 as Edward's health failed it became clear that Harold was acting as a second in command and carrying out many of the king's duties. This was done with such mutual understanding that in his closing years Edward regarded Harold as a son. It was a result of their relationship and their mutual confidence that when the end came for Edward he saw Harold as a right and proper successor.

Harold's relationship with William of Normandy was entirely

different. When they first met is not known with any certainty, but they must have been aware of each other for at least twenty years before the final conflict. Although they were fairly close in age William became Duke of Normandy in 1035, ten years before Harold was created Earl of East Anglia. From his appointment in 1045 Harold was almost certainly familiar with William's name, and as he became more and more familiar with Edward so he would have learned more about him.

Although it is possible that Harold and William could have met earlier they are known to have met in 1064 when Harold visited Normandy. By this time Harold, as Earl of Wessex, was a statesman and soldier of considerable experience. William was also an experienced statesman and soldier having been Duke of Normandy for nearly thirty years, albeit that some of these were when he was very young.

On the occasion of his visit in 1064 Harold met William as his liberator from the clutches of Count Guy of Ponthieu, by whom he had been imprisoned. If this was their first meeting then to some extent it could be said that Harold was at a disadvantage from the beginning. Because this visit by Harold had a considerable effect on the events that were to follow, it is worth considering the relationship of Harold with William during his stay in Normandy. If, as will be shown to be likely, Harold's landfall on the territory of Count Guy of Ponthieu was unintentional and Harold's party became the fair spoils of shipwreck, his position as the prisoner of Count Guy could have been very difficult but for the apparently generous intervention of William, albeit ultimately for his own ends. Although indebted to William for his release he was still technically a prisoner of the Norman Court. As part payment of his debt to William Harold took part in the Norman campaigns against Brittany for which services he was 'knighted' by William, thus making him William's vassal though it is questionable whether the duke of a small autonomous continental state actually outranks an English earl subservient only to a king. Probably as a condition of his release from Normandy Harold swore an oath to William promising to assist him to the English throne on the death of Edward. This was their last meeting before they joined battle at Hastings, and Harold must have left, when finally free to go, knowing he had sworn something under duress that was to separate their goals as long as they were both alive. Whether Harold had designs on the crown himself at this stage is uncertain, for his loyalties so far had been to the English Royal dynasty which had elevated him. What is certain is that he had a dislike of the Norman people and their ways, and could never envisage a Norman King of England with a Norman-dominated English society, particularly after the year's fiasco between 1051 and 1052. His dislike for William for having forced him to swear to try and achieve such rule must have been intense though at the time he could not afford to let his feelings show. From the release of Harold in 1064 these two men with their diverse qualities were becoming the main characters on the stage of Western Europe.

Harold's attitude to foreigners, however, was very different from his attitude to the Normans, and generally there was mutual respect in all his dealings. Although it has been claimed that his father, Earl Godwine, suffered from insular prejudice this was a time when Western Europe was opening up and insularity was not a quality a developing statesman such as Harold could afford to hold or indeed wished to hold.

Harold was a committed Christian. As a child and later as a young man Harold would have had considerable contact with members of the hierarchy both at home and on his journeys abroad. His dealings with individual clerics were almost invariably good, and some in particular became his close friends such as Wulfstan, prior and later Bishop of Worcester. Harold's attitude towards the Church was greatly influenced by his association with Edward who has been described as being more like a monk than a king, and this is substantiated by the endowment of the title of 'Confessor' and later by his canonisation by Alexander III in 1161. It would probably be true to say it was as much Edward's involvement with the Church as his failing health that made it necessary for Harold to assume the duties of kingship before Edward actually died.

It has long been held that Harold was more a friend of the secular clergy than the regular,[7] and while this may be substantially true it does not mean that he disliked monks. His greatest endowment to the Church was the foundation of a secular order of Canons at Waltham which had been given to him by the king. The abbey church there, dedicated to the Holy Cross, was consecrated by Archbishop Cynesige of York[8] in 1060 in the presence of Edward and his queen, together with Harold and Edith Swannehals and many dignitaries. Harold chose Adelhard as the first Abbot.[9] Waltham became a special place for Harold, not only was he the founder and chief benefactor but he had also collected relics from Rome for its endowment. It was to Waltham that he retired in times of need, as he did following his Welsh campaign and also before his battle with William. Finally it was to Waltham that Harold's body was supposedly brought for burial after originally being denied consecrated ground by William.

Harold also made endowments to other religious houses of which one was Peterborough. He had only one family connection with the Church and that was through his uncle Aelfwig who was made Abbot of Winchester in 1063.

During Harold's time as Earl of Wessex it became clear that Edward was unlikely to have a child, and Professor Freeman suggests that as early as 1057 Harold had designs on the crown.[10] Harold was a loyal subject of the king and to suggest that he had aspirations to kingship as early as that is unfair. The suggestion stems from the deaths in that one year of Earl Ralph, Edward Aetheling and Leofric. As Edward was without issue Ralph, Earl of Hereford, son of Edward's sister Goda and the French Count Dreux, would certainly have been a sound contender being the nephew of Edward and the grandson of Ethelred the Unready. Edward Aetheling had, perhaps, a stronger claim being the son of Edmund Ironside and also grandson of Ethelred the Unready but he had been banished when King Cnut succeeded Edmund

Ironside to the throne. The death of Leofric is also relevant as to some extent it weakened the House of Leofric and indirectly strengthened the House of Godwine.

With the two main contenders for the throne gone and the standing of the Godwines slightly enhanced, Harold's position as a possible contender must be acknowledged to have improved whether or not he had designs on the crown himself. It should be borne in mind that if Edward had promised the crown to Duke William of Normandy this was probably done in 1051 or 1052 during the banishment of the Godwines. In spite of their absence Harold was likely to have been aware of it, and if not would soon have learned of it upon his return. What he would also have known was that the crown was not Edward's to dispose of as he wished, that the succession required the full approval of the Witan and the English people and that Edward was free to change his mind about any bequest until his death. Nevertheless Harold would have been aware that William, being first cousin once removed from Edward the Confessor, was more than interested in the English crown. After the unpleasant experience the English nation had endured under the Norman magnates brought in by Edward during the Godwine banishment of 1051–1052, the enthronement of William is not something Harold would have wished on the English people.

Following the restoration of the Godwines in 1052 loyalty to the king had become paramount partly because Edward had banished nearly all the Normans and was displaying true confidence in the Houses of Godwine and Leofric, and partly because the country wanted no repetition of the Norman attempt to govern the country.

Harold, after succeeding to the earldom in 1053, functioned not only as Earl of Wessex but assisted Edward and busied himself in the defence of the realm from the incursions of Gruffydd of Wales in two campaigns.

Although he may have gradually become aware of the possibilities of ascending to the throne himself it seems more reasonable to interpret his actions as being aimed at making

England strong enough both administratively and militarily to withstand a Norman coup on the death of Edward. It is possible that the idea of Harold succeeding to the crown may have come from Edward himself.

Any idea that Harold's brother Tostig could have had an interest in the crown at any time before his expulsion from his earldom in 1065 must be discounted. Up to that point he had no quarrel with his older brother and would have been more interested in the house of Godwine and his own earldom than in aspirations to royalty. The situation altered with Harold breaking off relations with his brother and the king growing weaker. Tostig may at this stage have been jealous of Harold's position of strength but was probably no more than anxious to take revenge and regain his Earldom of Northumbria.

The only other contender was the young Edgar Aetheling, the son of Edward Aetheling who died mysteriously on his return from exile in 1057, and the great grandson of Ethelred the Unready. From the point of view of descent this lad, who was probably not much more than about twelve years old, had the best claim. However, although there were precedents of youthful responsibility at this time, his age was against him.

It may be that Harold as a confirmed patriot sought nothing else but the continuity of the English Royal dynasty through Edgar even until the dying Edward expressed a wish for Harold to succeed. It is worth emphasising the fact that although Edgar's father Edward died in suspicious circumstances in 1057 there is nothing to suggest that Harold was in any way involved in his death. Rather the opposite, had the later Norman writers wishing to denigrate Harold been able to accuse him of the murder of Edward Aetheling then they surely would have. This in itself may suggest the Normans knew something about it and perhaps may have been involved in an attempt to keep the field clear for Duke William of Normandy who believed he had been promised the crown in 1051, and whose chances of succession had been reduced by the return of Edward and his son Edgar from exile.

Thus Harold's standing in England prior to the death of Edward the Confessor, apart from his year's exile between 1051 and 1052, was very strong.

2

The Banishment and Restoration of the Godwines 1051–1052

The background to the banishment of the Godwines in 1051 lies deep in Edward the Confessor's early and formative years in Normandy and his resulting affinity with the Norman way of life.

It would have been unnatural if the English had not felt strongly against the Norman influence after the accession of Edward. Between 1042 and 1050 there were all the elements of a power struggle between Edward's Norman friends and the House of Godwine, and although the Godwines were growing in power to such an extent that in 1050 they were more powerful in earldoms than they were at the start of 1066,[11] they were not as well favoured at the Royal Court as they should have been because of the influence brought to bear against them by the Normans.

In 1051 things came to a head. The events which followed are of considerable importance in the animosity between the Saxons and the Normans, forming a part of the background to the Battle of Hastings and it is useful to consider them in detail. Edward the Confessor's brother-in-law, Eustace of Boulogne, who had become the second husband of Edward's sister, Goda, arrived at Dover with a band of compatriots from Normandy. They conducted their search for accommodation with the Norman arrogance so typical of their dealings with the Saxons, and one householder who resisted taking a Norman was wounded. He responded by killing Eustace's man and he was in turn killed on his own hearth by others of the band.[12] A skirmish followed in which about twenty townsfolk and many others were wounded. Florence of Worcester records that it was a Saxon who was killed first and that, following the Saxon revenge on a Norman, Eustace's men slew men and women and trampled babes and children under the feet of their horses.[13]

On seeing organised resistance Eustace of Boulogne immediately sought refuge and justice with his brother-in-law Edward the Confessor who was at Gloucester, and was warmly received, as no doubt was his prejudiced version of the events at Dover. Edward was angered by the apparent injustice done to the visiting Normans and ordered Earl Godwine to take retribution on the people of Dover. There can be little doubt that Earl Godwine, as Earl of Wessex, had heard the correct version of events before he received his instructions from Edward, and patently declined to inflict punishment or revenge on the injured parties at Dover. Godwine may well have guessed that Edward would have supported Eustace in a dispute of this nature and started to gather troops with Harold. In any event they both met Godwine's other son Swein at Langtree in Gloucestershire on 8 September, all with men from their earldoms.

The Earls Leofric of Mercia, Siward of Northumberland and Ralph the Timid, who was Eustace's stepson, met the king at Gloucester, and were willing to do battle with the Godwines at the king's request. The Godwines, however, were still patriotic and could see the harm that would be done to England by civil conflict, which would also weaken the Saxon cause *vis à vis* the Normans, and so sought peace with Edward requesting the trial of the Norman party of Eustace of Boulogne.

By now, under Norman influence, the Royal patience had run out and Godwine and his entire family had their possessions confiscated, were banished and given five days safe conduct to leave the country.[14] Godwine and his wife Gytha, Tostig and his wife Judith, the daughter of Baldwin IV Count of Flanders, Swein and Gyrth made their way to the South Coast, one version of the *Anglo-Saxon Chronicle* saying via Bosham and the other that they went to Thorney Island. They went as a party in great haste taking as much treasure as they could carry to Tostig's father-in-law Count Baldwin at Bruges where they stayed all winter.

Harold and his brother Leofwine made their way to Bristol to leave in Swein's ship which he had equipped and provisioned for himself.[15] It is apparent that Edward had second thoughts about allowing Harold safe conduct and despatched Bishop Aldred of Worcester with a swift body of horsemen to hurry after them and detain them on his behalf. It seems likely that Aldred did not like what was going on and was reluctant to execute the king's order, and in spite of a delay because of bad weather still permitted Harold and Leofwine to make their escape. They made their way in heavy weather with a few losses to Ireland, where they sought refuge with Dermot, King of Ireland.

So deep was the feeling that had been aroused against the Godwines at the Royal Court that Edward banished his Queen, Edith, to the care of his sister, the Abbess of the nunnery at Wherwell. She went with one female attendant but deprived of all her treasure. With the Godwine earldoms vacant Edward appointed Odda[16] earl of the four counties of the South West of Godwine's Wessex and Aelfgar earl of Harold's East Anglia.

Without the influence of the Godwine family at the Royal Court Edward was much freer in his choice of advisers and immediately increased the Norman numbers in his administration, which further alienated Edward from his Saxon subjects. These Normans totally failed to grasp any understanding of the Saxon way of life or system of laws and succeeded only in creating a great rift between themselves and the king on one side and the Saxon backbone of England on the other.

It was almost certainly at this stage that Edward intimated that Duke William of Normandy should succeed him as king, and as word of this spread the anger of the Saxons increased. It has been suggested that William visited Edward[17] during the Godwines' absence to have the succession confirmed, but it has been established beyond reasonable doubt by Professor Douglas that 'William never set foot in England before he landed here in 1066'.[18] It is possible that Robert of Jumièges went to Normandy at this time to indicate formally that Edward wished William to succeed him.[19] Nevertheless Edward was estranging himself from his loyal subjects who were becoming very disturbed by the injustice and lack of wisdom of the imported Norman overlords.

As Edward became aware of the alienation of his subjects he also found himself facing a challenge from Gruffydd of Wales who, in the absence of the Godwines, was much more of a threat, and in 1052 invaded Herefordshire where he slew many Normans and Saxons near Leominster, taking a lot of booty.

The matter of the succession, the oppression of Norman control and the threat of invasion from Wales gradually turned the tide of Saxon England in favour of the absent House of Godwine. There can be little doubt that the lack of understanding that the Normans had of the Saxon system and the poor rule as a result of it was something the Saxons could not bear to see perpetuated by a Norman succession, and it was because of this that when the Godwines returned in force later in 1052 the people were ready to welcome them back. Godwine had become the champion of the Saxon cause against the Normans.

It is likely that Godwine, knowing his people, may have anticipated their change of heart and made tentative preparations for a return.

The return of the Godwines began when a small collection of ships under Godwine himself sailed from the mouth of the River Yser on 22 June 1052, and after avoiding a small royal fleet landed at Dungeness and soon learned that the men of the home counties and South-East England would welcome the return of the Godwines and release from Norman oppression. Although he was pursued by the royal fleet Godwine escaped in bad weather and rode out the storm at Pevensey. Following this initial investigation and having canvassed support wherever he could, Godwine went back to Flanders knowing that England was ready for his return.

Whether there was any liaison at this time between Godwine

and Harold cannot be confirmed, although it would be naïve to think that they could have coordinated their return to England without messages going to and fro, although it is just possible that the two early raids were coincidental.

The royal fleet of forty ships[20] was not particularly well organised and morale was low, and the men were certainly not motivated against the Godwines. The South Coast, therefore, was substantially undefended and Godwine was aware of this.

Harold and Leofwine, having acquired ships and provisions during their stay in Ireland, entered the Severn estuary and made landfall near Porlock, probably in the bay between Porlock Weir and Porlock village where they encountered opposition from the men of Devon and Somerset. Had this been Harold's old territory the events may have been different, but he was not well known in the West and his attempt to live off the land caused anger among the people, making this perhaps the blackest moment in his career.

He considered it necessary to fight against his own folk in order to regain his position and that of his father, and to protect England from the possibility of a Norman succession. There was fighting near Porlock and 'more than thirty thegns'[21] were killed as well as many others. It is hard to understand what Harold was trying to achieve in a conflict of this size, and even more difficult to believe it was intentional. Both as a patriot and a conciliator Harold must have been very disturbed by the turn of events and it is likely that something had gone seriously wrong. It is possible that his search for support for reinstatement was seen locally as an invasion, or that some of Harold's men behaved in a similar way to the Normans at Dover the previous year. If this is true it was a bad mistake and it could easily be imagined why the local militia reacted as they did.

Having overcome this local resistance Harold resupplied his force from the locality and set sail west making his way round Lands End to join forces with his father.

Godwine must have made arrangements to be kept informed of events in the South of England because he heard fairly quickly that Edward's fleet had returned via Sandwich to London. The South Coast was now undefended and Godwine with a refurbished fleet made for the Isle of Wight, and while provisioning his fleet from there and Portland, patrolled the coast waiting for Harold and Leofwine to join him. After joining up they recruited along the coast and further inland wherever possible. The combined fleet then made for Sandwich collecting support in both ships and men from Pevensey, Romney, Hythe, Folkestone and Dover.[22] When the vastly increased fleet reached Sandwich Harold and Godwine were sufficiently confident to notify Edward of their presence.[23] Edward tried to raise an army against them but it is recorded that help came very slowly. He must have been aware that the Godwines could not have arrived with an army and that the majority of their strength must have come from the English side of the channel. He may also have become aware that the Norman influence was not going down at all well in England, and this was why the Godwines were getting such support. Godwine's fleet proceeded from Sandwich, still ravaging from place to place, round the Isle of Thanet into the Thames estuary and up the river to Southwark, arriving on Monday 14 September, where it waited for the tide. It seems likely that the Godwine's canvassing had prepared the people of Kent for his return as the fleet met no opposition on its journey to Southwark. While they were waiting Godwine 'treated the citizens so that they nearly all wanted what he wanted',[24] and when the tide gave them enough water they advanced through the bridge keeping to the southern bank and joined with the land force along the shore to face Edward's fleet and his army on the northern bank. This was an interesting confrontation as nearly all the opposing forces were Saxons and many of the more distinguished would have known and respected each other. Harold and Godwine asked for the return of all that was theirs, and at first Edward was reluctant. This angered their men but above all they would have had the one common desire with their adversaries – to strengthen England against foreign invasion. This could not be achieved by conflict and a truce was arranged, with the exchange of hostages, between Godwine and the king. Edward always strove for peace, almost at any price, and particularly on this occasion to avoid civil war among his own people. The soldiers were stood down on both sides and a meeting was fixed for Tuesday 15 September. This was to be a full meeting of the Witan convened by the king. Professor Freeman suggests that Godwine may have come ashore late on the Monday and spent the night in his house at Southwark.[25]

When the Witan assembled on the Tuesday morning harmony was quickly reached between Edward and the Godwines who were immediately released from their banishment and reinstated to their earldoms. The speed with which the settlement was reached indicates that Edward must have made up his mind to restore the Godwines to power well beforehand, and probably before he called up his apparently reluctant forces. However, in spite of acquiescing in the Godwines' wishes he still demanded hostages, and Harold's brother Wulfnoth and his nephew Hakon were surrendered to Edward who passed them to William of Normandy for safe keeping. In the reinstatement, Godwine, his wife and all his sons, except Swein who had not returned, were restored to their earldoms and possessions. The queen was also recalled to her royal position. Florence of Worcester records that the 'King and the Earl promised justice to all people'.[26] This is a strong implication that they both understood justice to have been absent in the law and its execution during the year of Norman administration. In order to achieve this justice it was necessary to remove those Normans who had been assisting the king in government, and in the event many of them fled for fear of reprisals for what they had knowingly done against the Saxons. The *Anglo-Saxon Chronicle* relates that Robert of Jumièges, Archbishop of Canterbury, Bishop William of London and Bishop Ulf of Dorchester escaped with difficulty, which implies that there were many Saxons who would have liked to deal with them in their own way. Robert fled in such haste that he left without his pallium – his insignia of office from the Pope.[27]

Edward, in spite of the mass expulsion, did keep a few of his more trusted Norman friends, and Bishop William of London was reinstated after a short time. Two Normans, Osbern and Hugh, surrendered their castles and were allowed by Leofric, Earl of Mercia, free passage to Scotland. The property of Robert of Jumièges and Ulf of Dorchester was divided between Godwine, Harold and Queen Edith.[28]

Those Normans who remained in England after the mass expulsion were Ralph the Timid, Edward's nephew who was son of Goda and Dreux and the second cousin of William of Normandy, Robert the Deacon, Richard son of Scrob, Oufroy, who was an equerry to Edward the Confessor and Herman, Bishop of Wilton.

With the return of Saxon administration and the restoration of the Godwines to their earldoms, Aelfgar had to stand down in favour of Harold as Earl of East Anglia. This he did freely, knowing that he was likely to succeed to Mercia on the death of his father Leofric, and probably because he was as anxious as the Godwines to see England restored to Saxon control.

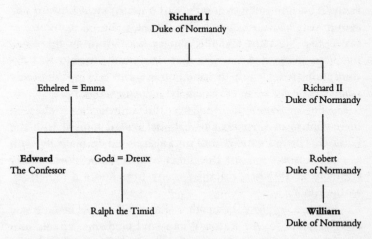

Table showing connection between Edward the Confessor and William, Duke of Normandy

Following the return of the Godwines Edward must have been pleased to re-establish his friendship with Godwine and Harold in particular. He may well have realised the errors of the previous year and perhaps resented the advantage the Normans took of his friendship.

By the tenth year of his reign Edward was becoming much less interested in the running of his country and rather more involved with the Church. Without any formal arrangement he allowed the administration of government, with the exception of official regal duties, to pass to the Godwines. This was a good practical working system that well suited both the king and his Saxon subjects.

The expulsion of Robert of Jumièges from Canterbury, while imperative at the time of the restoration of the Godwines, was to create more problems than were foreseen at the time. Banished from England he could no longer function as Archbishop of Canterbury, but he had not been deposed by the Pope. In replacing him as Archbishop of Canterbury with the Godwines' friend Stigand, Bishop of Winchester, Edward was filling a post that was not vacant, and making an appointment that was not likely to be confirmed by the Pope. To some extent Edward was acting in defiance of church law. Because the relationship between the Normans and the Papacy was strong at this time, the Pope supported the Norman cause and Stigand was excommunicated. Clearly the situation was viewed very differently when Edward was canonised in the following century.

During the remainder of the year the Godwines re-established their control of England and Edward busied himself with the Church. The dramatic year of 1052 also closed dramatically with a violent storm on 21 December which 'blew down many churches and houses, scattered many trees and tore others up by the roots'.[29]

The year 1053 saw the death of Earl Godwine. The king was at Winchester for the Easter Witan, and Godwine, Harold and Tostig were with him. At a meal they were all attending on the Easter Monday 12 April Godwine collapsed and lost his 'speech and all of his strength'[30] suggesting some sort of a stroke and he was taken to the king's chamber where it was hoped he would recover, but he made no improvement losing the little strength he had left and finally died on Thursday 15 April, and was buried in the Saxon minster at Winchester. With the Witan still assembled Harold was appointed to the Earldom of Wessex and Aelfgar returned to East Anglia.

3

Harold's Visit to Normandy and the Oath of 1064

There are only three contemporary sources for the visit made by Harold to Normandy in 1064. These are the accounts of events as recorded by William of Poitiers[31] and William of Jumièges,[32] and the pictorial account of the Bayeux Tapestry, all of which relate the Norman side of the story and are presented with almost transparent bias. The English writers are silent on the matter making no reference to the visit at all, and the *Anglo-Saxon Chronicle* is strangely blank for the whole of the year 1064.

That a visit took place is not open to question, but the reasons for the visit are still a matter of some conjecture. William of Poitiers and William of Jumièges are both clear in indicating that Harold was sent by Edward the Confessor to confirm a promise made by him in 1051 that on his death William would succeed to the Crown of England. This theme is perpetuated by the Bayeux Tapestry where it forms the first part of the pictorial story. The opening scene shows Edward instructing Harold to go to Normandy with his message, and this is followed by Harold in prayer at Bosham Church and a feast in his manor there. They are then seen boarding ship and setting sail. The crossing ends in a windy landing and the immediate arrest of Harold by Count Guy of Ponthieu. He is taken to Beaurain, and after payment of a ransom, is handed over to William. Following his reception at William's palace he may be seen taking an active part in William's campaigns in Brittany against Duke Conan, and for his efforts Harold is knighted. The party then returns to Bayeux where Harold is dramatically shown taking an oath of

Harold, Earl of Wessex, on his way to Bosham at the start of his fateful visit to Normandy in 1064

fealty to William after which he is released and allowed to return home. William of Poitiers places the oath-taking at Bonneville-sur-Touques, which is now generally accepted as being the correct location.[33]

Despite the strength of these Norman accounts much historical opinion has suggested that Harold's visit was involuntary
and that the circumstances which brought him to Normandy in
1064 were other than an instruction from Edward the Confessor.
After the year of Norman administration between 1051 and 1052
it became clear that there were wide cultural differences between the Saxons and the Normans, and after the restoration of
the Godwines the Saxon culture was preserved, and the rift
between the Kingdom and the Duchy grew wider. Probably
because of this and the resentment the Normans felt towards the
Godwines following their return to power in England, Harold
chose to avoid Normandy on his visit to Rome in 1056.

It has been suggested that Harold's landfall on the territory of
Count Guy of Ponthieu was the result of being blown ashore
and shipwrecked during a fishing trip; however, it is quite
possible to be blown ashore on a favourable beach without
wrecking the ship. As the landing was in Ponthieu, and involuntary on that particular coast, it would have been customary for
Harold to become Count Guy's prisoner, and his property
Guy's booty. For this to have happened it is possible that
Harold was on his way to Flanders.

The other possibility is that Harold was on a mission to
negotiate the return of his brother Wulfnoth and his nephew
Hakon who had been given to William as hostages on the return
and restoration of the Godwines in 1052. By 1064 William
realised that Edward was becoming old and was confident that
the crown would pass to him. Harold, not having made public
any aspirations to the throne, although he did not wish William
to succeed, probably had no fear of him and felt safe in making
overtures personally for the return of his brother and nephew. If
this was the cause of the visit then Harold could also in this case
equally well have finished up being blown ashore without shipwreck on the coast of Ponthieu.

It must remain purely a matter of conjecture as to whether
Edward saw Harold as his successor at this time. If he did, then
the Norman presentation of the visit in terms of a message

concerning the succession would be a complete fabrication, and the oath taken under duress presented as freely made.

Objective assessment of the circumstances would not preclude a visit of Harold to William as an emissary of Edward to confirm William's succession, though it is inconceivable that Harold could have wished it. Alternatively it is perhaps more likely that at this stage in his reign Edward saw a Saxon succession as more desirable with the young Edgar Atheling as king and Harold as regent. In this case Harold's visit could only have been made deliberately, and perhaps unwisely, in order to obtain the release of Wulfnoth and Hakon. If Harold's visit was unintentional then it can only have been the result of being blown ashore on the coast of Ponthieu and captured by Count Guy. If this latter is considered realistic then Harold is likely to have been on his way to Flanders and the Court of Baldwin V, Tostig's father-in-law, at St Omer.

The weight of evidence would seem to be against Harold's travelling as an emissary of Edward because as such he would have been covered by diplomatic immunity. If this was the case it is extremely unlikely that William would have paid any ransom to Count Guy for his release and, as payment was made,[34] it must be construed that Harold was on a private visit and regarded, following his landfall in Ponthieu, as 'fair game' by both Count Guy and William.

Whatever the background to the visit, there is little cause to doubt the authenticity of the Tapestry in placing the embarkation of Harold at Bosham, or the subsequent details of his sojourn in Normandy.

The following events as depicted in the Tapestry show Harold's arrest and transfer to 'Belrem' now Beaurain near Montreuil. After negotiations Harold is surrendered to William at Eu on the Normandy Ponthieu border. This is followed by a scene where Harold is shown either delivering a message to William or perhaps negotiating about Wulfnoth and Hakon. Harold may then be seen assisting William in his campaign in Brittany and for his services he is 'knighted' by William. This ceremony probably took place immediately after the surrender of Dinan, following which the party returned to Bayeux where the Tapestry places the 'oath'. Harold then returns to England and reports to Edward.

During his time in Normandy Harold at the least had some interesting experiences. As well as his arrest, which was probably his first and only experience of imprisonment, his rescue by William and the much publicised oath-taking, there are other aspects of his time in Normandy worthy of consideration. In William's campaign against Brittany Harold saw Avranches, Mont St Michel, the River Cousenon, Dol, Rennes and Dinan, and although he was under 'open arrest' as William's prisoner his conditions matched his standing as an earl and his relationship with William was superficially very good, partly because William did not see him as a threat at this time. He was treated as a member of William's household and became very friendly with William's wife Matilda, even perhaps to the extent of being considered suitable as a husband for their daughter, Aelfgiva. According to Thierry William used to retire early leaving Harold talking to his wife Matilda.

It is clear from the Tapestry that the Normans wished it to be known that Harold played a substantial part in the Brittany campaign as he is shown rescuing fallen Normans from the River Cousenon, and after the surrender of Dinan he is knighted by William. The implications of this ceremony have been considered in connection with Harold's personal relationship with William. This tribute by William may have been endowed on Harold as a result of a special act of bravery at Dinan because this is where it is shown on the Tapestry to have taken place. Alternatively as the fall of Dinan marked the end of the campaign it might be regarded as a campaign award rather than an acknowledgement of a particular act. Whatever the circumstances of the giving of arms '*dedit arma*' it has a relevance in Harold's relationship with William. In accepting the honour Harold is to some extent accepting publicly his subservience to William. Some significance may be drawn from the sequence of these events as depicted on the Tapestry, because immediately following the gift of arms at Dinan and the return to Bayeux Harold is shown making his oath, which may perhaps be seen as part of the submission that started at Dinan.

Harold was personally very much against William succeeding Edward to the crown of England, and there is little to suggest that he had any personal aspirations of his own at this time. All the evidence points to the oath having been taken under duress, his reluctance stemming from a burning desire to keep the Normans out of England for the Saxon Royal house.

The oath as depicted on the Tapestry shows Harold with arms outstretched each touching a reliquary. One reliquary may be clearly identified by the handles used for carrying it in processions. The other, on the altar which may be identified by the altar steps and the altar cloth, is in the form of a tabernacle. This tabernacle would also have contained relics as it was not customary for the reserved sacrament to be kept on the altar at this time.[35]

Harold had no knowledge of the contents of these caskets and this is emphasised by the poet Wace who claims that Harold was staggered when the covers were removed.[36] They contained the bones of two British saints, Ravennus and Rasyphus.[37] The circumstances suggest that the whole event was very much a stage-managed affair, and must have taken place in a church or a chapel for there to have been an altar. The fact that the relics were of British saints can hardly have been fortuitous and were probably selected by William to have maximum effect on Harold. Even though there is every indication that the oath was taken under duress, Harold's personal feelings, when it was revealed on whose bones he had sworn, must have been very mixed. However, he never let the oath worry him to any great extent because he never deemed it necessary to seek dispensation from the Pope as the circumstances made the oath itself totally invalid.

The terms of the oath as recorded by William of Poitiers are that Harold swore to be William's representative at Edward's

court for as long as Edward remained alive, to strive to achieve
William's succession to the throne, to maintain a garrison of
William's knights at Dover Castle and elsewhere, and provision
them. These terms in themselves, if accurately recorded, are
unrealistic in so far as it would have been impossible for Harold
to have maintained Norman knights in England under Edward's
rule and there was no way the Saxons would have permitted
their fortresses to have been surrendered to William's men. In
making the oath Harold must have been fully aware that he
would have been totally unable to fulfil any part of it until
Edward was dead. This no doubt was something of a relief for
although the oath was being made under duress there was little
chance of any confrontation about its invalidity for the fore-
seeable future, that is until the death of Edward. William would
have understood Harold's position and probably expected no
immediate results. Nevertheless, because he believed he had
been promised the throne by Edward, he may have considered
it possible to have Norman garrisons in England.

Although Harold had a definite dislike of the Normans and
their way of life this did not stop him making a substantial
contribution to William's campaign in Brittany, which may have
increased William's confidence in him. Indeed William may not
have seen him as a threat at this stage at all, and probably
envisaged Harold continuing as Earl of Wessex after his own
coronation. If this was true it was certainly naïve on William's
part, firstly in underestimating Harold's loyalty to his own
countrymen and secondly in his assessment of the Saxon people.

There is also the suggestion of an arranged marriage between
Harold and Aelfgiva, one of William's daughters. Whether
Harold promised to marry her (as she is shown on the Tapestry
after Harold's meeting with William at Rouen during the visit of
1064) as part of the oath is very much open to conjecture, but the
many references to some arrangement afterwards suggest at
least that this possibility was considered, and at the most that it
formed part of the oath. If the latter was true then Harold may
have chosen to disregard it completely on the grounds of the

invalidity of the oath, or because his responsibilities at home did not give him time to organise the marriage before Aelfgiva's death,[38, 39] which was sometime before that of Edward the Confessor.

The application of the oath by William was a very polished piece of political manoeuvring, for whether William expected Harold to keep his word or not, he had made sure it was public knowledge throughout the courts of Western Europe so that Harold would be compromised.

The reasons for the *Anglo-Saxon Chronicle* being blank for 1064 are not clear but it seems unlikely that it could have been connected with Harold's absence or his oath. As a point of interest there is no contemporary English reference to the oath perhaps because Harold made it known that as it was taken under duress it was invalid and therefore irrelevant. Whatever the feeling was on the English side of the Channel and it certainly may be regarded as being opposed to the Normans, William must have been reassured by the support of Harold's oath because all the Saxon magnates who were said to have supported Edward's promise of 1051 were now dead.

After the oath had been taken the next scene in the Tapestry suggests that Harold was immediately permitted to return home, and he is recorded by William of Jumièges as being sent home with many gifts[40] as well as his nephew Hakon,[41] who with Wulfnoth had been surrendered to William as a hostage guaranteeing his succession after Edward's promise of 1051. Wulfnoth, Harold's brother, was not released, perhaps to ensure fidelity to the oath.

The scene depicting the return to Edward shows Harold in a rather peculiar stance, almost as if he was a hunchback. The meaning of this is not clear. Possibly it is meant to show his embarrassment at having been caught and compromised by William, but this is not something the Normans would have wished to portray and could only be true if surreptitiously done by the Saxon embroiderers.

4

Harold's Election and Succession to the Throne

After the restoration of the Godwines in 1052 the bond between the family and the king became very deep. After the death of Earl Godwine in 1053 there is enough evidence to suggest that of his children Edward befriended Harold and Tostig and regarded them as the sons he never had, and it was only two years later that Tostig was elevated to being Earl of Northumbria. While there is also evidence to suggest that Tostig was Edward's favourite[42] it is likely that Edward was aware of Tostig's weaknesses and his impetuous and greedy traits of character, and if not, would soon have heard the rumblings of dissatisfaction during his rule of Northumbria.

Harold's relationship with Edward after Godwine's death matured on a personal level and established itself on a firm professional level as well. As Earl of Wessex Harold would have spent a lot of time with the king, and in any event was never very far away when Edward needed advice and support. It was in this way that Harold became Edward's second in command.

The Welsh wars certainly raised Harold's standing and popularity and, as Sir Frank Stenton suggests, he reached a point where he was beyond rivalry at the royal court.[43] His position even then was somewhat unusual and this was not missed by the people of the time. In the Tapestry he is entitled '*Dux Anglorum*', and Florence of Worcester refers to him as '*sub regulus*', both of which suggest a position nothing short of royal deputy. The strength and importance of Harold's position, however, was not only dependent on his personal standing with the king, but also to a great extent on public opinion and his acceptance by the people, and it was probably not until the last eighteen months of Edward's reign that Harold reached the level suggested. It was probably after his return from Normandy in 1064 that the possibilities of succeeding Edward became a reality in his mind. Freeman observes that Harold's way to the crown was strangely cleared of all obstacles,[44] but this in no way implies any intrigue on his part. The death of Edward the Confessor without issue should not in itself have caused a breakdown in the Saxon Royal line, but the fact that it did was almost certainly circumstantial. Alfred, Edward's brother, had been murdered thirty years earlier and whatever the motivation was for that crime, it could not have been connected with Edward's absence of issue as he was not at that time king. Twenty-one years later Edward's nephew Earl Ralph,[45] the son of Goda, died and in the same year Edward Aetheling, the son of Edmund Ironside, and half nephew of Edward the Confessor, also died, but in this case the circumstances were a mystery and have remained so. As has been suggested there is the possibility of Norman involvement, but it seems certain that Harold had no part in it and the reasons for this have already been considered.

With the field of right and proper contenders for the throne so dramatically reduced towards the close of Edward's life only the young Edgar Aetheling had any hereditary claim.

It would be naïve to think that Harold did not recognise this situation, but he may not have regarded himself as a suitable successor until he realised Edward the Confessor would die before Edgar Aetheling was old enough to take over.

The point at which Harold actually saw the crown as being within his grasp cannot be known, nor can it be known what his motives were in trying to achieve it. Certainly he was personally ambitious, but whether these personal ambitions were a greater influence in his seeking the crown than his desire to keep out the Normans is very much open to question. The other factors which affected this issue were the wishes of the dying king and the attitude of the Witan. The bequest of the throne was not within the power of the king[46] but it is known that Edward suggested Harold as his successor to the Witan and Thierry quotes no less than six sources.[47] Edward had been king for more than twenty years and his peaceable justice and wisdom were well respected and this would have had a great influence on the Witan.

Harold had become something of a national hero after his success in the Welsh wars and was well accepted as Edward's deputy both at home and abroad. Harold, also, would not have been without favour with the Witan of which he was the foremost member, and it should not be overlooked that he would have been instrumental in its composition. Any suggestion that the bequest was made under duress seems unlikely in the light of the relationship between Edward and Harold, and unreasonable as a dying man has little to lose.

Because the bequest of the crown was not within the power of the king the final decision of the Witan would supersede any improper bequest of 1051 to William. What is certain is that Edward did have influence with the Witan immediately before his death, and also that the Witan made its views known to Edward.

The decision to appoint Harold as Edward's successor was reinforced by Edward's deathbed bequest which is recorded by Florence of Worcester[48] and which Professor Freeman claims was too well known to have been denied.[49]

Edward died on 5 January 1066 probably with the senior members of the Witan around his bed, and it is likely that Harold was one of them. The scene is depicted in the Tapestry.

Events moved very quickly after Edward's death, and while the final burial arrangements were being made the Witan would have been resolving the succession. Having discussed the matter at length previously, and being unable to select from the Saxon Royal House their duty was to appoint from without, and in so doing the deathbed wishes of the king would have become much more significant. At this juncture the Witan would have been concerned about continuity of rule because without it William would surely assume the crown on the grounds of the promise and Harold's oath. To avoid this their action had to be swift. Whether Harold was present at his own selection is not known. He may very well have stood down as his ability and willingness to accept would have been well known to the Witan, and his popularity in the country was not open to question. The appointment was almost a foregone conclusion, probably just a formality, and so it was that Harold, Earl of Wessex, without any Royal descent, succeeded to the throne. He was the free choice of the Witan and the people of England. As it was normal for the coronation of a king to follow immediately upon his election, Harold's coronation immediately after the burial of Edward may not have seemed untoward to the people of the time, though it must be stressed that very swift action was required to maintain political stability. It is interesting that the Tapestry depicts these scenes out of chronological order. The scenes of the laying out and burial of Edward's body precede the death scene, and this may well have been done so that the coronation of Harold might be placed next to the death scene in order to suggest that Harold snatched the throne with improper haste.

The burial of Edward was the first major public service to be conducted in the new abbey of Westminster which had only been consecrated a few days before on 28 December. The second event was the coronation of Harold on the same afternoon, and this was conducted by Archbishop Aldred of York,[50] the Primate of Northumberland. The choice of ecclesiastical authority for this ceremony was probably made by Harold himself in order to eliminate any accusation of invalidity that might have been raised if the excommunicated Archbishop of Canterbury, Stigand, had been chosen to preside. Not only had he been excommunicated by five consecutive Popes[51] but the fact that he had received his pallium from the usurper Pope, Benedict X, could be regarded as nullifying his authority. The fact that William of Poitiers relates that Harold was crowned by Stigand may be confidently dismissed as an attempt to prejudice the validity of the coronation. William of Poitiers was a Norman favouring the Norman cause, whereas Florence of Worcester was an English monk and historian writing objectively, with, according to Professor Freeman, scrupulous care knowing the hostility of the Norman writers, and anxious that the truth be made clear.[52]

The Norman view is also implied in the Tapestry which shows Stigand next to Harold when he appears on the throne immediately after the death of Edward, the clear implication being that the excommunicated Stigand presided at the coronation.

Harold was the first king to be crowned at Westminster. In the ceremony he was anointed with holy oil, had a sceptre placed in his right hand, an orb in his left, and a crown on his head.[53]

Ironically it was to be the same very Saxon Aldred, who had been a monk of Winchester, Abbot of Tavistock, Bishop of Winchester and finally Archbishop of York, and a good friend of the Godwines, who crowned William and Matilda, also at Westminster Abbey on Christmas day in the same year, 1066.

So it was that Harold at the age of forty-five, the son of a freebooter Viking, without any hereditary claim and against all the odds, reached the highest position in the land, a land for which he was to give his life defending it against the invader.

News of Harold's coronation reached William within a few days, probably relayed to Normandy by some of the very few Normans who had remained in Edward's service. He received the news while hunting in the Quévilly forest and returned immediately to Rouen. He was extremely angry on three counts. He had been foiled in his attempt to acquire the English throne, he had been ridiculed by this failure in the eyes of other European heads of state, and he was infuriated by the oath breaking of Harold, whom he regarded as a vassal. It has been suggested that the latter point, namely a breach of faith by a vassal, angered William as much, if not more, than Harold's oath breaking and acceptance of the crown.[54]

From the moment William knew that Harold had been crowned the confrontation between them was confirmed, and from this point it is clear that William had grossly under-estimated Harold. While William very much resented the open defiance of someone he had come to regard as a vassal he was probably equally annoyed with himself for his very naïve as-sessment of Harold's character. It must have come to him as something of a shock to realise that he had failed completely to compromise Harold into accepting an oath taken under duress. He also underestimated Harold's loyalty to the Saxon people, which in these events was apparent from its strength. It does seem as if William had been unaware of the procedure in the Witan for the succession to the Saxon crown in the event of the king dying without issue. He may have thought he had arranged things in his favour from his dealings with Edward in 1051 and Harold's oath of 1064, but failed to realise that the bequest was not in the power of the king.

William of Poitiers's account of the succession of Harold is ostentatiously biased, recording his seizure of the throne, his breaking of the oath, his haste which denied public choice and his coronation by the 'unhallowed' Stigand. Professor Freeman refers to the Norman claims as being prejudiced, vague and ambiguous.[55]

William's first and immediate reaction on hearing the news was to despatch emissaries to Harold requiring him to relinquish the crown and conform to the terms of his oath. This must have been done in the full knowledge that it was unlikely to succeed, and was probably no more than a diplomatic exercise by William so that he was seen to have tried diplomatic channels to resolve his claim before resorting to invasion. Needless to say Harold dismissed the emissaries and according to William of Jumièges he 'not only disdained to listen but seduced all the English people away from obedience to the Duke'.[56]

From the moment of his acceptance of the crown Harold must have been aware of the considerable dangers that were likely to accrue as a result.[57] Of these, William's personal anger and desire for retribution were not the only problem. William's standing in Western Europe had been improved by the deaths of the King of France and the Count of Anjou,[58] his main enemies. Harold also faced a threat from Harald Hardraade of Norway and Swein, King of Denmark[59] and the possibility that Harold's ousted brother Tostig might join with any invading force.

In general the dangers stemmed from the publicity William had given the oath and the fact that Harold's case was not represented at the papal hearing. Harold was in a difficult position. Either he could challenge the validity of the oath which would have given some credibility to William's case, or he could choose to ignore it, which is what he did. Had he decided to challenge William's claim he would have found William's witnesses lined up against him testifying to his oath, and because of the stage management of the event he would have been unable to substantiate the matter of duress.

Harold knew that the oath, made under duress, was null and void and saw no reason to seek any dispensation. What he did not appreciate was that because of William's skilled application of the oath hardly any European of consequence was going to understand the circumstances of the oath let alone believe in Harold's case. This point is borne out by the doubts supposed to have been expressed by Harold's brothers just before the Battle of Hastings when they offered to do battle on his behalf to forestall any further aggravation over the oath.[60] However, this is a Norman account and its objectivity is open to question.

One other problem also faced Harold at this time. He was not readily accepted by the Northumbrians as their king and because Mercia was in the hands of Edwin, the brother of Morcar of Northumbria, the loyalty of Mercia must also have been slightly suspect.

In order to cement the allegiance of these two earldoms Harold married Ealdgyth, the sister of Edwin and Morcar, shortly after his coronation, and to some extent the ploy was successful. Ealdgyth had been the wife of Gruffydd of Wales whose head Harold had taken to Edward the Confessor in triumph to mark the end of the Welsh wars. Harold had enjoyed a long-lasting and sincere relationship with Edith Swannehals who had borne him five children though he had never married her. He should have given up this association on his marriage, but he had not quarrelled with Edith and she was the mother of his children, so it was a matter of some doubt whether he ever seriously intended to sever this relationship in favour of his marriage. Although it seems Ealdgyth bore Harold two sons, Ulf and Harold, albeit posthumously and therefore twins, it was Edith Swannehals who identified Harold's body after the Battle of Hastings.[61]

In an attempt to improve the allegiance of the Northumbrians Harold went to Northumbria with Wulfstan, Bishop of Worcester, who pointed out that allegiance to Harold was better than the return of Tostig and persuaded them to accept Harold as their king.

With his country united behind him Harold was prepared to face the dangers that he knew would come from beyond his shores.

5

Harold's Short Reign

Harold was very much aware of the dangers from abroad on accepting the crown and must have looked immediately to the defence of his realm. He had first to consider all possibilities of likely invasion and then consider the condition of his own defences. The kingdom was an island and this was his best defence. He was fully aware that William was bound to invade but this would take time to arrange. The more imminent danger was in the North of England from Harald Hardraade of Norway and Swein of Denmark, though Harold would have had little idea of their intentions or the possibility of any collusion between them. What he did know was that Harald Hardraade had a fleet and could invade at almost any time, and that if he came it was probable that he would attack in the North. The other element of danger was the exiled Tostig. Though there was little damage he could do on his own, he was certainly able to initiate activity on the part of others and assist them with whatever support he could muster. When Tostig was exiled in 1065 it is unlikely that Harold foresaw that he would make trouble after his accession, as it is far from certain that he saw himself succeeding Edward at that time. However, by the time he became king he may have been concerned about any alliance that Tostig might establish with William.

To counter these possible invasions Harold had a regular army of over three thousand housecarls and could call on a further ten thousand fyrdmen.[62] The fyrdmen were the territorials of the time, the part-time soldiers who were liable for forty days' training each year. They were not as well equipped as the regular housecarls as they did not usually have access to hauberks or kite-shaped shields. In comparison their skills were limited, coming for the most part from their training, but a proportion of them would have gained valuable experience in the Welsh wars.

The army was paid for by a war tax levied from the villages at two shillings a hide, which in effect took over from the Dane-geld.

Harold also inherited Edward's fleet and there were tentative arrangements with certain ports and sailors on the South Coast to provide what amounted to a Sea-fyrd.[63]

This was Harold's military strength at his succession and in view of the dangers that he anticipated he was anxious to improve that strength right from the start of his reign. Professor Freeman suggests that he may have had some difficulty in persuading others of the urgency of the situation. Harold did achieve some improvement and probably felt capable of count-ering invasion from Harald Hardraade and William provided they came at different times. If they came at the same time, he would then have to leave the defence of the North to Edwin and Morcar but, while their loyalty was no longer in question, their ability and determination as generals and the strength of their armies were uncertain quantities.

While the defence of the realm was of paramount importance to Harold it was far from being his only concern. Florence of Worcester relates that on becoming king he 'immediately began to abolish unjust laws and to make good ones, to patronise churches and monasteries, to pay particular reverence to bishops, abbots, monks and clerks, and to show himself pious, humble and affable to all good men'.[64] It seems from this that during the latter years of Edward's reign things had been allowed to run down a little and although Harold had been closely involved with Edward he had been busy fighting the Welsh wars and during 1064 had spent time involuntarily in Normandy. Now he had the opportunity to put some of the things right.

As Florence records that Harold's actions of reform were 'immediate' following his coronation it may be confidently accepted that he set these reforms in motion before he went north with Wulfstan to establish the loyalty of the northern earls. It is likely that Harold spent as much as two months in and around London and the South Coast establishing his southern defences and modifying his laws before he felt able to visit the North.

It is recorded in the *Anglo-Saxon Chronicle* that he returned at Easter which in 1066 was on 16 April.[65] The Easter meeting of the Witan, the Gemot, which took place at Westminster was in session from 16 to 23 April,[66] and there can be little doubt that much of the agenda was taken up with the defence of the realm. One item that was not a matter of defence was the appointment of Thurstan as Abbot of Ely, and this Professor Freeman records as being the last peaceful event of 1066.[67]

Sir Frank Stenton makes the point that few memorials of civil government can be expected to survive from Harold's short reign[68] and of those that do by far the most important is his coinage. Harold established mints throughout the whole of England and is known to have had forty-five different mints each obtaining their dies from London, and this in itself suggests continuity of administration[69] and a strong central control.

It was because of his time as Edward's right-hand man that Harold was able to wield his authority with such close direction. His ability came from knowing the ropes as much as the strength of his character, and the fact that many of the magnates and senior administrators were his own appointments.

It was while Harold was establishing and consolidating his position as king that William was manoeuvring to destroy it. During the first few weeks of Harold's reign William started his military and logistical preparations for invasion, and initiated his shuttle diplomacy with the Pope and princes of Europe to strengthen his position using Gilbert, Archdeacon of Lisieux, as his emissary. This resulted in Harold having no allies across the channel,[70] and although he was fully aware of this he was not particularly concerned because he trusted only in himself and his island realm.

It was the day after the close of the Easter Gemot, on 24 April, that Halley's comet first appeared in the sky 'such as had never been seen before'.[71] It must be stressed that this coming of the comet was many times brighter than the 1985/6 appearance because in 1066 it passed between the Earth and the Sun rather than round the far side of the Sun as it did in 1985/6. In 1066 it appeared shining brightly at night in the southern quarter of the sky.

The people of the time were not well informed in the astronomical sciences and were substantially alarmed by their heavenly visitor. It shone, according to Florence of Worcester, for seven days with decreasing brightness,[72] and this is confirmed in the *Anglo-Saxon Chronicle* where it is referred to as the 'long haired star'.[73] Although tradition has it that the comet was seen by the superstitious people of the time as a bad omen for Harold there is little evidence to support this. Its depiction on the Tapestry carries the caption *'Iste Mirant Stella'* – these men admire the star – there being no suggestion of warning or evil foreboding, but rather the recording of a significant contemporary event.

During the next two months Harold was busy consolidating his defences and guarding his coast with an innumerable army[74] to counter the invasion he now knew would come from Normandy. This he had established by sending spies across the Channel to the mouth of the Dives on the Cherbourg peninsula to assess the size of William's army and fleet.[75] One spy was captured and returned to Harold by William with a message threatening his invasion within a year.[76] There are also suggestions that during this time William was endeavouring to mislead Harold by feeding misinformation to him through Baldwin of Flanders,[77] and this may well have been something to do with Tostig, his son-in-law, who had taken refuge with him in Flanders when he was banished in 1065.

There was, however, in Normandy some resistance to

William's intention. Many were simply afraid partly because they did not think William could mobilise a strong enough force to succeed and partly because they knew the strength of Harold's defences. William, however, listened to none of this because he felt that with the anticipated foreign support he could succeed, his anger and desire for vengeance against Harold becoming something of a personal vendetta.

The threats from abroad and the defences would have been well aired at the Easter Gemot, and it was within a month of this meeting that Tostig invaded the Isle of Wight with a force of Flemings and as large a fleet as he could muster, and money and provisions were given to him.[78] Florence of Worcester presents the facts slightly differently saying that he made the islanders pay tribute.[79]

After this Tostig moved east along the South Coast doing damage wherever he could,[80] commandeering a small fleet in Sandwich harbour, conscripting some of the sailors and accepting the help of others. While he was in Kent he was joined by Copsi, one of his supporters from Northumbria, who came from the Orkneys with seventeen ships,[81] which brought Tostig's fleet up to one of sixty ships. Harold on hearing of Tostig's attack on Sandwich immediately set out to counter it only to find that the fleet had moved on just before he got there.

Tostig, anxious to cause as much trouble as he could, then ravaged the area around the mouth of the River Burnham in Norfolk,[82] meanwhile Harold having assembled his fleet at Sandwich sailed to the Isle of Wight to guard against the inevitable invasion by William.

Tostig moved further north, entered the Humber estuary and was defeated by Earl Edwin while ravaging the south bank, where he burnt villages and killed many men,[83] and Edwin's brother, Morcar of Northumbria, fended off any attempt to land further up the coast. It was probably lack of success that led the southern sailors to desert the invaders and return to Sandwich, so with only twelve ships Tostig sailed north to summer in Scotland with Malcolm Canmore, King of Scots.[84]

Now that any immediate threat from Tostig was over Harold was free to 'distribute his land force at suitable points along the sea coast'.[85] This he did, probably east from the Isle of Wight where any attack from William was more likely. It was the start of what was to be a long defensive watch, and one that William of Poitiers later recorded as being executed with 'insensate zeal'.[86]

This force would have been made up of sections of the Fyrd and probably certain units of housecarls to provide some leadership and backbone. For a wait of any length the matter of supply becomes much more important, and Professor Freeman makes the point that they could not live off the land in their own country[87] and must therefore have had the support of the people. It would not have been too much of a burden on them as the troops were well disciplined along the length of the coast and demands would have been light.

Harold and his men waited and watched throughout the summer of his reign convinced that the greatest danger was from William and he was resigned to leaving the defence of the North to Edwin and Morcar.

By the end of August Harold was fairly confident that William would not be coming that year, and although he may still have been inwardly worried, he stood down his army on 8 September and disbanded the Fyrd. This is not something he would have done if he had thought there was any likelihood of attack from Harald Hardraade in the North, so it seems that he had dismissed that from the 1066 calendar as well.

The Fyrd would have made their way back to their own villages to assist with the collection of the harvest, and this is almost certainly the reason why the traditional date for the standing down of the Fyrd was 8 September.[88] At the same time as he stood down his army Harold directed his fleet, which was also guarding the South Coast, to London and some ships were lost on the way.

There is a legend that after Harold returned to London he fell ill, and that he went to his foundation at Waltham Abbey to pray before the Holy Rood. Abbot Aethelsinge spent a night in prayer on his behalf during which he had a vision of Edward the Confessor who instructed him to tell Harold to be strong in battle against his enemies.[89] The message was delivered, and Harold seemed to recover from his ailment.

It was probably shortly before Harold stood down his army that Tostig submitted to Harald Hardraade in Scotland and, according to the *Anglo-Saxon Chronicle*, became his vassal.[90] Florence of Worcester records that Tostig joined him at the mouth of the Tyne 'according to previous arrangement',[91] though it is possible that this arrangement was made in Scotland only slightly earlier.

The suggestion has been made that news of Harald Hardraade and Tostig reached Harold early in September,[92] and that this is why he moved his fleet to London. This is unlikely to be correct because if it was true Harold would never have stood down his army. Harald Hardraade was definitely not expected when he actually arrived.[93]

The precise date that Harald Hardraade and Tostig started their attack on the north-east coast of England cannot be known with any certainty. Communications were reasonably good at that time and it is quite possible that Harold learned of their attacks on Cleveland and Scarborough as early as 15 September[94] shortly after he had returned to London and before he got news of the defeat of Edwin and Morcar at Fulford.

Harald Hardraade and Tostig had entered the Humber Estuary and sailed up the Ouse as far as Riccall on their way to York. They would have been unwise to proceed further as the Wharfe joins the Ouse just west of Riccall and their ships could have been cut off by the fleet of Edwin and Morcar which was on the Wharfe at Tadcaster.

Harald Hardraade and Tostig were met by Edwin and Morcar at Gate Fulford on Wednesday 20 September. Edwin and Morcar's loyalty to Harold was not open to question as they fought hard against the invaders for most of that day and conceded victory only after sustaining heavy losses. The battle was fought on the north bank of the Ouse and although many of the Vikings were killed, the Saxons were unable to prevail and the survivors fled, many being drowned in the Ouse.[95]

After the battle, York was an open city to the invaders and it was surrendered with hostages and substantial booty to Harald Hardraade by its leaders who also undertook to help him against Harold.[96] The city was left intact by the Vikings possibly because of its willingness to surrender, but more perhaps because it had very deep Viking roots as it had been under the Danelaw for many years, and for that reason may have had a greater affinity with the invaders than is generally appreciated.

It seems almost certain that Harold knew of the invasion well before the defeat at Fulford and because of this was partly mobilised and ready to march northwards on the day of the battle or even earlier.

Having sent urgent word to all quarters that he needed as much support as could be mustered to join him on his dash north, Harold set out with the army he had with him on what must be regarded as one of the greatest marches in history. The actual date he left London is uncertain. It has been suggested that he could have heard about the coastal attacks in the North as early as 10 or 12 September[97] though it is questionable whether Harold was actually back in London by that time, and perhaps a more likely date would be 14 or 15 September which allows time for his visit to Waltham. Although this reduces the number of days that he had to reassemble his army, it still allows five which should have been sufficient to bring the main force together.

When he was satisfied that he had sufficient numbers and that he was sure of gaining strength on the way northwards Harold left London sometime between Monday 18 and Wednesday 20 September on a forced march of 180 miles. This was a remarkable feat in which an army with full equipment, some on horseback and many on foot, covered a minimum of thirty-seven miles a day for five days, or if they left on the Wednesday rather than earlier, an amazing forty-five miles a day for four days. This would not have necessitated travelling at night as eight hours marching at five miles an hour would be all that was required, and even this could have been eased considerably if they travelled for the eleven hours of daylight with only short breaks for refreshment. Messengers would have gone ahead of the army to warn of the crisis and get the townsfolk and villagers *en route* to prepare what food they could spare as refreshment and sustenance for the passing troops.

Their route would almost certainly have taken them up the line of the Great North Road, but what the quality of this road was like after six hundred years of neglect is a matter of conjecture. It has been suggested that it was wide enough for sixteen horses abreast,[98] but this can only have been true in some short sections. What would have happened to the deteriorating surface would have depended on the amount of wear and to some extent its distance from the nearest towns. Along sections that had been well used large potholes would have appeared in the Roman metalling, and by avoiding these traffic would have widened the clearance of the route. Where this happened there may well have been enough width for sixteen horses abreast but hardly otherwise. Other sections, particularly in wooded areas, may have been almost completely overgrown. In conditions such as these the rate of progress would have been very irregular. Although not recorded Harold's route was almost certainly through Braughing, Godmanchester, Peterborough, Lincoln, Doncaster and Ferrybridge to Tadcaster, where he arrived late on Sunday the twenty-fourth. Here the army camped for the night about twelve miles south-west of York.

After receiving the capitulation of York Harald Hardraade and Tostig may have returned to Riccall where the wounded and much of their equipment would have been taken after the Battle of Fulford,[99] but on Monday 25 September they were at Stamford Bridge about eight miles east of York with the major part of their army. Their reasons for being there are not known with any certainty. The *Anglo-Saxon Chronicle* records that it was to Stamford Bridge that hostages were to be brought,[100] and it has been suggested that if the landowners of Yorkshire chose, or were forced, to provide for the invading army, then this was a sensible military choice as it was the centre of a good road network at the time.[101] Not only could supplies and horses be brought from the surrounding area to this central assembly point, but it also gave Harald Hardraade certain useful options for movement afterwards.

Harold and his army spent the night at Tadcaster perhaps suspecting that the Norwegians were still in York completing their negotiations. Early on the morning of Monday 25 September, probably at first light between 5.30 and 6.30 a.m. Harold led his army out of Tadcaster towards York arriving at about 8.30 a.m. perhaps anticipating an encounter. The city was undefended and the Vikings, Harold discovered, were at Stamford Bridge. In an attempt to maintain the advantage of total surprise Harold 'went right on through York'[102] and the first indication the Vikings had that Harold was anywhere in the vicinity was when his army appeared over the top of the slight slope that runs down from Gate Helmsley to Stamford Bridge, and the time was shortly before noon.[103]

The only detailed account of the Battle of Stamford Bridge of any age is the one by Snorri Sturlasson, the Icelander who recorded the Norse sagas almost two hundred years afterwards. This account carries all the embellishments that might be expected in sagas handed down by word of mouth for so many years, and carries some confusion with the Battle of Hastings which followed only nineteen days later. Some of Snorri's detail, therefore, is open to question[104] though other points of interest suggest that a substantial part of his story is accurate.

It would have taken a few moments for the significance of the arrival of Harold's army to register among the rather dispersed and resting army of the Vikings along the banks of the River Derwent, and a little longer to make an appraisal of the size of the English army and the impending threat. Once assessed, terror must have replaced complacency in the Viking army as they tried to assemble and position themselves on the south side of the river, and this they would have done by way of the only bridge which they defended thus allowing their men time to form up before the Saxons broke through and crossed the river. There is a vivid description in the *Anglo-Saxon Chronicle* of a Norwegian who bravely defended the bridge and was only removed by a Saxon who floated under the bridge on an improvised craft and stabbed him 'under his corselet' with a sword or spear.[105] This cleared the way for Harold's army to surge across the river.

There are accounts of a discussion between the leaders before the battle but these are unsubstantiated and might be regarded as unlikely in the circumstances of the unexpected arrival of the Saxons. Traditionally King Harold offered Harald Hardraade a little in excess of seven feet of English soil, as he was a tall man, and F. W. Brooks suggests that the Icelandic sagas from which this story comes are more likely to be correct on points of detail rather than the topography and incidents of the battle.[106] It may be that Harold did make such a comment, but it is more likely to have been an aside to one of his own men rather than a direct threat to Harald or Tostig.

The struggle for the bridge may well have lasted long enough for Harald Hardraade to form up his army on the slightly higher ground known as Battle Flats.[107]

The battle was in three phases and although the details of the formations and fighting are rather obscure, the first of these was the initial encounter once the whole of the Saxon army had crossed the bridge. By this time the Norwegian army and its allies would have been drawn up in close formation awaiting the Saxon attack. Although Harald Hardraade had one of the best and most feared armies in Europe at this critical moment it was divided. About one-third of their force, which included the wounded from the Battle of Fulford, had returned with much of the equipment to their base at Riccall, thus leaving the remaining two-thirds ill prepared for battle.

In spite of these disadvantages and Harold's surprise arrival they bravely fought off the initial Saxon attack, but it was during this fierce encounter that Harald Hardraade was killed. The Norwegians rallied under Tostig for the second phase of the battle which lasted well into the afternoon. It was during this time that Tostig was killed. When the Saxons had first appeared, Harald Hardraade had sent messengers urgently to Riccall calling all able-bodied men to the battle with as much equipment as they could carry. The men at Riccall were under the command of Eystein Orre, and would have come at full speed. Their arrival in the second half of the afternoon would have been a welcome sight to the flagging Norsemen discouraged by the loss of Tostig. The third and last phase of the battle has become known as 'Orre's Storm'. The men that Orre brought from Riccall, of which the number is not known with any certainty, would have travelled carrying their armour rather than wearing it. When they arrived they cast it aside because of the heat, and perhaps because of the amount of time it took to put on, and went berserk into the fray of battle – berserk originally meaning without armour. It was a wild and probably somewhat uncoordinated attack by men who were exhausted after their rush from Riccall, and may have been more tired than the survivors they had come to help. However, their arrival boosted the morale of the Vikings, alarmed the Saxons and extended the battle by something in excess of an hour. This final phase lasted until early evening by which time any resistance had been totally destroyed. Harald Hardraade, 'the greatest warrior under heaven',[108] lay dead and with him the greater part of his much feared army. He had been out-generalled and caught completely off guard as a result of Harold's decisive action and his incredibly swift march north. However, Harald Hardraade had been called to fight rather sooner than he would have wished after the hard battle at Fulford only five days before.

It was probably Olaf, the son of Harald Hardraade, who finally conceded defeat and conducted the negotiations for the safe withdrawal of the survivors. It may also have been Olaf who despatched Paul, Earl of Orkney, with a small force to guard the ships[109] which had been virtually unattended since Eystein Orre's dash to Stamford Bridge.

The slaughter at Stamford Bridge was enormous, the Vikings losing something in the region of five thousand men, and the Saxons, although victorious, probably losing about two thousand men. These figures are speculative but reflect consideration of the numbers of men thought to have been present, the size of Harold's army which afterwards made up the core of his force at Hastings, and finally the record that only 24 ships were required by Olaf to transport the Viking survivors home.[110]

Harold must have been saddened by the loss of so many of his good men, and also the loss of his brother on the other side. Although Tostig was killed his two sons, Scule and Ketel,[111] Harold's nephews, survived and probably returned to Norway with the remnants of the Viking army as they later settled and founded families there.[112]

Harold bore no malice after his victory at Stamford Bridge and displayed the magnanimity that might be expected of a king who had successfully defended his realm against a foreign invader. After making the Viking survivors swear oaths for peace he allowed Olaf, Paul, Earl of Orkney and their bishop to return home[113] with their survivors.

Harold took the body of his brother Tostig and had it buried at York.[114] The body of Harald Hardraade was buried on the battlefield but a year later was transferred to Nidaros in Norway.[115]

The booty from the destruction of the Viking army was substantial, and probably because he realised that it would be very useful in the inevitable encounter with William, Harold broke with tradition and decided not to share it out among his men.[116]

F. W. Brooks suggests that the terms for the release of the Viking survivors were negotiated on 26 September which was probably the day that Harold returned to York. In spite of the fact that Harold had stood down his South Coast defences against William's invasion he seems to have been anxious to return south as soon as possible and may have remained in York only one or two days.

After his lengthy delay in Normandy William arrived with his army on the morning of Thursday 28 September, and it is estimated that the news of his landing could not have reached York before 1 October.[117] However, as William's invasion was seen as inevitable a system of beacon fires may well have existed, and it is possible that the news reached York as early as the morning of 29 September.[118] Florence of Worcester records that Harold was told that William had arrived with a 'countless host of horsemen, slingers and footsoldiers and help from all parts of Gaul'.[119] Professor Douglas suggests that Harold may well have been on his way southwards when the news reached him, and if this is so then it makes his arrival in London on 6 October all the more plausible in terms of time and distance.

From the moment Harold knew that William had landed the buoyancy of his victory at Stamford Bridge would have disappeared and the old anxiety would have returned with a desperate urgency. The one thing he had hoped to avoid had happened; the defence of his realm had demanded the impossible, that of being in two places at the same time. As a result William was free to consolidate his bridgehead, and this he did with his usual ruthlessness, killing, burning, and destroying to terrorise the local populace into submission. This kind of action had been observed by Harold when assisting William in Brittany in 1064, and would have greatly increased his sense of urgency.

Because Edwin and Morcar had been defeated at the Battle of Fulford, Harold left the North in the care of Sheriff Marlswegen,[120] and possibly as early as 30 September started his march south. The urgency of the departure cannot be known unless it is established whether Harold knew of William's landing before he left or not. If he did get the message before he set out, the contingent leaving York was likely to have been larger as Harold would have rounded up every available person. Had he learned of the landing *en route* the pace would have quickened and a new call to arms would have been rushed to all who could help.

6

William's Preparations

The news of Harold's coronation made William extremely angry. He consulted his half-brothers Odo, Bishop of Bayeux, and Robert de Mortain, who were the legitimate children of his mother Herlève[121] and her husband Herluin Vicomte de Conteville, and resolved, according to William of Poitiers, to avenge the insult by force of arms and win the kingdom by war.[122] The fact that William of Poitiers mentions the matter of insult indicates clearly how William of Normandy felt; it was a matter of personal honour.

He called together a council of war of all his vassals and advisers to sound them on their support for an invasion of England.

This meeting took place at Lillebonne[123, 124, 125] and among members of this council, according to William of Poitiers,[126] were Robert de Mortain, Robert Count of Eu, Richard Count of Evreux, Roger of Beaumont, Roger de Montgomerie, William fitzOsbern and Hugh the Vicomte. These and William's other vassals in Normandy were obliged by terms of their feudal tenure to provide him with knights, men, arms and equipment in stated quantities in times of emergency, or when he planned expeditions to subdue adjacent territories. William must have known that two problems faced him: first, that none of his vassals was obliged to provide men for service overseas and secondly, that, even if they did all they could, it was doubtful if between them they could raise a force large enough not only to overcome Harold's army but to subdue the rest of England as well. At this stage, the armies of Edwin and Morcar were still undefeated.

The members of this council were much against what they saw as a foolhardy proposition. To invade Britain would involve an expedition of a size they had not assembled before and the successful shipment of that force across the Channel with all its impedimenta. So as a body the council, though with some dissenting voices, turned down the proposal on the double grounds that they were not obliged to provide for services overseas and that the element of risk was too high. The meeting ended in disorder, which angered William and confirmed his determination to get what he wanted. He had failed to rally the military support he needed and felt insulted a second time by the unwillingness of his vassals to avenge Harold's affront.

William would not have survived as an independent ruler from the early age of eight had he not been under the guidance of experts in the political intrigues of the time. He had learned these arts well, as already illustrated by his administration of the oath to Harold. He had been almost continuously at war or facing rebellion since he assumed power but his resourcefulness and his powers of persuasion were far from exhausted. By direct and personal interview with his vassals one at a time,[127] by encouragement, cajolery, and promises of conquered land, he was able in the end to persuade them to promise double their prescribed quotas. Even so it seems unlikely that he could raise within his Duchy more than 1,200 knights,[128] and it was essential therefore to gain support from outside the Duchy as well.

To achieve moral approval for his proposed invasion, and get the military assistance he needed from the other countries in Europe, his cause had to be seen as righteous. To this end William despatched emissaries to Pope Alexander II,[129] reporting Harold's treachery and requesting the blessing and support of the Church for his intentions. It was not an easy decision for the Pope – the political implications were considerable[130, 131] – but Alexander II was a former pupil of Lanfranc, William's trusted adviser, to whose pleading he must have given a favourable ear. At any rate, he did in the end give his blessing. (The fact that Archbishop Stigand of Canterbury had been excommunicated by five successive Popes for usurping his position may have helped in making the decision.)[132] A consecrated banner[133, 134] was sent to William with full Papal approval for military action. Obtaining Papal approval for his cause was a particularly adroit piece of diplomacy. Pope Alexander was induced to take sides in a dispute where the rights and wrongs were uncertain. Once William had his approval the expedition became a crusade, morally demanding the support, if not the practical military assistance, of all the Christian nations of Western Europe.

As a result of this, pledges of support for William were greatly increased. The Emperor Henry IV promised German help,[135] Sweyn of Denmark pledged support,[136] and backing from William's neighbouring provinces improved. Large numbers came from Brittany and Flanders, slightly fewer from Artois and Picardy, but there was little response from Maine and Anjou and only nominal assistance from Champagne, Poitou and Apulia.

At this stage it was too early to assemble the men for a marine invasion; there were as yet no ships. However, knowing something of the amount of support he was likely to get, William was able to prepare and assemble a Channel fleet. It was made up of existing craft – which did not amount to very many – supplemented by a large number constructed specially for the purpose. Robert Wace, writing some while afterwards, claims that out of 752 ships ordered 696 were delivered. This figure is probably high and a figure in the region of about 500 is likely to be nearer the truth,[137] but this was still a massive undertaking. The style of these craft was based on the contemporary longship or drakken; sometimes these vessels reached 150 feet in length.[138] The Gokstadt ship, which was a merchant vessel, was only 76 feet in length and 17 feet wide[139] and it has been calculated that it could carry 32 oarsmen as well as a similar number of passengers.[140, 141] The largest ship in the Icelandic sagas carried 34 pairs of oars. The size of each of William's ships may not have exceeded 80 feet, but shipbuilding skills were clearly available.

The detailed design of William's craft is not known with any

Norman ship of the traditional Viking pattern. Note the high stern and prow, single sail, steerboard and oar holes

certainty, and the best indication comes from the Bayeux Tapestry. Their shape was certainly of the traditional Viking pattern with high sweeping bows and stern, and a deck at water level throughout with a continuous row of oar ports.[142] The keel may have been slightly less pronounced than the traditional Viking pattern as these vessels were designed for the single purpose of crossing the Channel, and a flatter bottom would have facilitated beaching on a hostile shore. There seems, however, to have been no intention to row across the Channel, which would have reduced the number of knights and horses that could be carried. The Tapestry illustrates the single large sail, oar ports and the steerboard, or large paddle-like oar used for steering and positioned near the stern on the starboard side. As with the other pictures in the Tapestry there is little attention to scale.

It has been suggested by Freeman[143] that the following people provided ships, though his figures, which total 782, are unrealistic:

> Odo, Bishop of Bayeux
> William fitzOsbern (the first to offer)
> Roger de Montgomerie
> Roger de Beaumont
> Hugh d'Avranche

Hugh de Montfort
Gerald the Seneschal
Walter Giffard
Vulgrin, Bishop of Le Mans
Robert de Mortain
William d'Evreux
Robert of Eu
Remigius

William's own ship was given to him by his wife Matilda and was named *Mora*.[144] It was fitted with a brazen child with stretched bow in the prow, and an effigy of Robert of Normandy in wood on the sternpost.

The construction of these 500 ships, at numerous sites, took up the months of early and mid summer of 1066 and involved a vast and carefully organised coordination of supplies and craftsmen. Clearly there was no time to use seasoned timber and the Tapestry shows the preparation of the rough timbers and partly assembled ships.

Hauberks, suits of chain mail, suspended on poles, being carried towards the ships for loading

Northern France and the South Coast of England

The Tapestry gives a clear pictorial account both of the loading and the equipment and supplies involved. Hauberks, or suits of chain mail, were carried between two men on poles. Hand carts are shown loaded with arrows, helmets and a barrel of wine. Men may be seen carrying swords and lances, and there is a bearded axe. Other men are carrying a barrel and a sack, presumably of flour. Apparently, therefore, all necessary military equipment was loaded, and also an initial supply of food to cover the soldiers' needs until a bridgehead could be established. After a foothold had been gained, either with or without a battle, the invaders could then live off the land.

William also brought with him three castles. The Norman castle at this time was a strong wooden structure usually placed on top of a large mound or motte functioning as a keep. These structures were brought over as prepared fitting parts and could be quickly assembled as required when a suitable mound had been located or constructed. The parts were held together by wooden pegs which were brought over in barrels. The construction of one of these mottes is shown on the Tapestry.

Thus, on or about 12 August,[145] with the men and ships ready and the equipment and supplies assembled at the mouth of the Dives, between the Seine and the Orne, William and his fleet were ready to sail but the wind was unfavourable. William had to wait and also maintain the morale and fitness of his men.

7

The Norman Crossing

On 12 September[146] William moved his fleet from the mouth of
the Dives, where it had been delayed for a month because of the
wind, to St Valéry at the mouth of the Somme. Whether he
intended originally to make his crossing from Dives is not clear.
The crossing from St Valéry was a great deal shorter and the
longer crossing would have made it very difficult to avoid being
sighted in daylight before landing. By starting from St Valéry,
William had a much better prospect of a crossing in darkness for
a surprise arrival at dawn. However, it was impossible for so
large a number of men and ships to embark and cast off in
darkness and this part of the operation had to be done in
daylight. Even if embarkation were finished as late in the evening as twilight allowed, given a fair wind it would still have been
too early to sail directly across. A landfall on the English coast
before dawn would not have been possible without mishap. The
fleet would have to assemble offshore, after loading, and wait at
anchor until the signal was given to proceed. Getting nearly 500
ships afloat and under way all at the same time would have been
almost impossible, quite apart from the risk of accident and
collision.

It was fortunate for William that he had the help of Baldwin
of Flanders, his father-in-law and first cousin, because it ensured
the ports in Northern France were friendly.[147] He therefore had
a wide choice of points nearer the English coast. He chose St
Valéry which was very suitable both for reassembly and re-
embarkation, on the land of Count Guy of Ponthieu. To get
there from Dives involved a journey in coastal waters only, and

it was a good point for joining with forces from Picardy and Eastern Normandy.[148] One of the reasons for the move of the fleet from Dives to St Valéry may have been that food supplies had become critical as a result of the long wait for a favourable wind. The transfer of the fleet also provided valuable experience in the transport of horses which was a fairly new skill for the Normans and the experience gained in Sicily between 1060 and 1061 with Byzantine instruction was obviously useful.[149]

This move from the Cherbourg peninsula to St Valéry was not without incident and William of Poitiers indicates that as well as losing some ships in bad weather, which was seen by some of William's men as a bad omen,[150] there were some cases of desertion, probably because of the long wait and the shortage of supplies. The Duke increased the daily ration, and had the dead from the shipwrecks buried secretly at St Valéry.[151] He then had the bones of St Valéry himself paraded for the veneration of the troops,[152] both to distract them from the business of waiting and to maintain their morale.

William's arrival at St Valéry on 12 September[153] was followed by yet more waiting and he continued to have problems with the morale of his troops. He exhorted them and ordered constant prayers for a favourable wind to avoid further delay. Eventually the wind changed and the final loading of the vessels and embarkation of men and horses took place amid a great flurry of activity which probably lasted most of the afternoon of 27 September. William of Jumièges implies that the hauberks and helmets were already on board.[154]

The transportation of the horses presented special problems. It would have been unwise to crowd horses together in one ship for fear of losing a large number, and it is more than likely that they were dispersed through the fleet with perhaps not more than ten in any one ship. Horses in transit, particularly in unstable vehicles, require a good deal of support and this was probably achieved either by closely placed stall bars padded with bags of straw, or by packing the horses tightly together to support each other. Whatever the method used, great care

The masthead lantern on William's ship

would have been needed, as horses cannot be sick; they may suffer colic or abdominal discomfort and become so distressed as to die. Generally, however, they travel well and being embarked for only a little over twelve hours on a journey that seems to have been fairly smooth it is unlikely that many were lost.

The ships assembled offshore as light faded, each with a lamp, and awaited the signal from William's ship, the *Mora*, which could be identified by its masthead light. A trumpet gave the signal for the fleet to sail and William, leaving his Duchy in the care of his wife Matilda,[155] weighed anchor somewhere near midnight. During the night his ship, perhaps because it was not carrying any horses,[156] somehow drew ahead of the remainder of the fleet and at first light could see nothing astern but sea and sky.[157] William immediately cast anchor and had a good meal with wine issued to all on board. Then lookouts from the mast saw first of all a few ships and afterwards 'numberless masts' on the horizon. After regrouping, the fleet made landfall between 8.30 and 9.30 a.m.[158] in the sheltered bay of Pevensey. The coastline is no longer as it was then,[159] since the eleventh century the sea has receded, and the rivers have altered their courses. Modern maps give a very distorted impression of the very favourable harbour facilities then available to William.

Only two ships were lost in the crossing – one of them carrying William's soothsayer, who failed to foretell his own disaster.[160] Of these two it is possible that one came ashore near Romney and was dealt with by the locals.

THE NORMAN LANDING

The ships seem to have beached at Pevensey in line abreast. After unstepping the masts to improve stability on the beach, the most urgent task must have been to unload the horses, for whom the journey may have been something of an ordeal. Before this could be done in safety, however, it would have been necessary to send scouts inland to test resistance and ensure that a bridgehead could be gained. Although William must have known that Harold had stood down his full army on 8 September, when the Fyrd duty terminated, he certainly expected some organised military resistance to his landing. It is extremely unlikely that he knew of Harold's dash to the North to counter the invasion of Harald Hardraade of Norway and Tostig.

William of Malmesbury records that William missed his footing as he stepped from his ship, the implication being that he fell. A nearby soldier quickly turned what could have been seen as a bad omen to advantage by exclaiming 'Comrade, you hold England, O future King'.[161]

Initially William was probably surprised by the lack of opposition, but it would not have taken him long to find out where Harold had gone and take immediate advantage of his absence. The residents were in no position to resist, and would have been particularly unwise to try, as their strength must have been extremely low after the recall of the Fyrd to meet the invasion in the North.

After the unopposed landing, William had one of the three portable castles hastily erected within the Roman fort at Pevensey.[162] The following day, 29 September, he moved to Hastings but not without testing the local resistance further and making his presence felt throughout the locality. He used patrols, we are told by William of Jumièges, consisting of about twenty-five knights each. One of these was led by Duke William himself and on one occasion it had to return on foot because of the rough nature of the ground. William was recorded as having returned carrying the heavy hauberk of William fitzOsbern as well as his own,[163] and this may have had something to do with William fitzOsbern's knowledge of the locality. Without his hauberk he could have conducted his scouting much more efficiently.

At the time of the transfer of William's army to Hastings, which is shown on the Tapestry, the English were seeking sanctuary in the churches when their homes were destroyed by the invaders.[164] The Normans in their present mood, however, had little respect for the churches, which they defiled,[165] performing acts of vandalism and destruction hardly consistent with the crusading nature of their invasion – but entirely in keeping with the Norman practice of lowering the defenders' morale by creating alarm and despondency. This was something that Harold had experienced at first hand while assisting William in Normandy in 1064. It was to have a great effect on his decisions about when and where to fight.

Construction of a motte for a wooden castle. Note the layers of soil, contemporary pointed spade, small shovel and Papal banner used for encouragement

As William did not know in advance where the fleet would make its landfall, his choice of Hastings as the headquarters of his bridgehead was likely to have been made on intelligence reports from the brothers William and Osbern fitzOsbern[166] on the topography of the region. Hastings provided a geographically defensible position protected to some extent by the now dried-up lower reaches of the rivers Brede and Bulverhythe on the flanks, and a beach from which a defended retreat could be made should the need arise;[167] it was to this beach that William transferred his fleet. Hastings afforded direct access to London along an established route if the military situation demanded it, though any immediate advance on London does not seem to have been part of his plan; indeed after the battle he went to some lengths to avoid the city, being uncertain how he would be received. There were also roads from Hastings to both the east and the west.[168]

On arriving at Hastings William had the remaining two wooden castles erected, possibly in the Roman fort there,[169] though it has been suggested that a lower-lying site may have been chosen.[170] It was two days after William's arrival at Hastings, probably on 1 October, that Harold was told of his landing.[171, 172]

8

The Norman Army

In order to invade another country with any chance of success it is generally accepted that the invading army should be considerably in excess of the defending force, and William's attempts to achieve this have been discussed.

The actual size of William's force has been the subject of much research and conjecture. Cumulative opinion based on independent assessments of both the circumstances and the logistics suggests that the number of fighting men was likely to have been in the region of 5,000,[173] though there could have been as many as 2,500 more, made up of boat crews, supply personnel, stable lads, maintenance men and servants, many of whom would have joined the ranks of the infantry.

The figure of 5,000 combatants has been reached in different ways, one being based on the time it took to embark[174] and supported by the average crew of a Viking ship. It assumes a fleet of 450 ships and is consistent with the troop movements of Robert of Gloucester in 1142,[175, 176] though the twelfth-century Norman poet Wace puts the figure at 696.[177] Other calculations start from the number of knights that the Normans themselves were actually able to put into the field. This would be about 1,200,[178] supplemented by another 800 from adjacent and supporting countries. This latter figure is higher than might be expected and was the result of Papal support and the crusading nature of the expedition.

The size of the body of archers and infantry was related to the number of cavalry, as many of the knights brought soldiers with them. The total figure generally accepted is in the region of

William, Duke of Normandy, with his half-brothers, Bishop Odo and
Robert de Mortain, at Hastings before the battle

between three and four thousand, depending on how many of
the boat crews and service personnel took up arms.

How the complete force was loaded into the ships is a matter
of conjecture, as neither the loading figures nor the number of
ships are known with any degree of accuracy. No attempt to row

across the Channel can have been intended as is shown by the long wait for a favourable wind. This suggests a crew of about five, of whom at least two needed previous sailing experience. In an attempt to estimate the number of ships and their loading, two conjectural patterns are given, on the assumption that the knights brought up to 500 spare horses and that about 100 ships would have been required as supply vessels to carry the food and military supplies.[179] The difference between the patterns covers the possibility that on this unusual crossing each horse may have been cared for individually – one man to one horse – which may well have been the only way of controlling frightened animals at sea.

FIRST CONJECTURE

Ships		Horses	Knights	Infantry	Crew
250	×	10			5
143	×		14	21	5
100*	×				5
493		2,500	2,002	3,003	2,465

SECOND CONJECTURE

Ships		Horses	Knights	Infantry	Crew
357	×	7	6	1	5
75	×			35	5
100*	×				5
532		2,499	2,142	2,982	2,660

* = Supply vessels

These figures are purely speculative but they do suggest that unless the basis of the maximum of ten horses or thirty-five men per vessel is substantially altered – and there seems no good reason for that – then the number of ships is likely to have been in the region of 500, a figure reached separately. Whether or not the knights or grooms travelled with their horses, one to one, makes little difference. What is initially a surprise is that about 2,500 crew were required to ferry the invading force across the Channel. Probably most of these were also infantry and others were shipmen or menials. What is certain is that no unnecessary personnel would have been permitted to accompany the expedition.

Among the infantry must have been a substantial number of archers, though the precise proportion of archers to heavy infantry is uncertain. It seems unlikely that they exceeded about 800, but this figure would have outnumbered the Saxons, whose ranks were diminished by the Battle of Stamford Bridge and the march both ways.

Thus it seems likely that William's force was made up of approximately: 2,000 cavalry; 800 archers; 3,000 infantry; 1,000 sailors and supply combatants.

Those who accompanied William who are identifiable beyond reasonable doubt are, in relation to the size of the force, remarkably few. Some imaginative and indeed fictional lists have been produced, but they are derived from the 'Roll of Battle Abbey' which is now generally accepted as a heraldic fiction. Those people who were definitely present on William's expedition to England in 1066 have been identified by Professor D. C. Douglas as follows:[180] Aimeri, Vicomte de Thouars; Engenulf de Laigle; Erchembald, son of Erchembald the Vicomte; Eustace, Count of Boulogne; Geoffrey, Bishop of Coutances; Geoffrey, son of Rotrou; Gerelmus de Panileuse; Gulbert d'Auffay; Hugh de Grandmesnil; Hugh de Montfort; Odo, Bishop of Bayeux; Ralf de Tosny; Roger, son of Turold; Robert of Beaumont; Robert fitzErneis; Robert de Mortain; Robert de Vitot; Taillefer; Turstin, son of Rollo; Vitalis; Wadard; Walter Giffard; William Malet; William d'Evreux; William fitzOsbern; William de Warenne; a member of the House of Ponthieu. To these must be added the name of Humphrey de Tilleul en Auge, established as being present by J. F. A. Mason.[181] Five other names are also included as being extremely likely to have accompanied William, though their presence cannot be categorically confirmed. They are: Gerald the Seneschal; Hugh d'Ivry; Richard fitzGilbert; Rodulf (Ralf) of Tancarville; Pons.

Certain biographical details of some of these people are known. *Aimeri, Vicomte de Thouars*, was probably a member of William's original council of war; *Engenulf de Laigle* is recorded by Ordericus Vitalis as having been killed in the battle. *Eustace, Count of Boulogne*, was the son of Count Guy of Ponthieu who had captured Harold in 1064. He was a brother-in-law of Edward the Confessor, and it has been suggested that he was one of the knights who slew Harold.[182] He brought knights on the campaign, possibly carried the Papal banner at certain stages and was seriously injured in the closing stages of the battle.[183]

Geoffrey, Bishop of Coutances, is recorded by William of Poitiers as having taken part in prayers before the fighting.[184] *Gerelmus de Panileuse* is known to have joined the expedition, as gifts to Holy Trinity, Rouen, were confirmed by his brother after his death in the battle.[185] *Gulbert d'Auffay*, a descendant of Richard III of Normandy, was a relation of Duke William, being his first cousin twice removed; Ordericus Vitalis's statement of his presence at the battle is likely to be correct as Ordericus and Gulbert's brother Hugh were monks together at St Evroul.[186]

Hugh de Grandmesnil, a soldier and politician of considerable standing who functioned in both Britain and Normandy after the Conquest,[187] is recorded by William of Poitiers as taking part in the battle.[188] *Hugh de Montfort* (sur Risle) is also recorded by him as being there and possibly took part in the slaying of Harold.[189] It is also known that he brought a troop of knights from his manors near the River Risle.[190]

Odo, Bishop of Bayeux, was William's half brother, being the legitimate[191] son of William's mother Herlève and Herluin, Vicomte de Conteville. He was consecrated Bishop of Bayeux at the age of fourteen, and his military prowess matched his ecclesiastical standing. His contribution at Hastings is probably over-emphasised by the Tapestry, possibly because he was responsible for the Tapestry's design. Other contemporary references to his activities in the battle are remarkably few.[192] However, his presence at Hastings is unquestionable: he not only took part in prayers beforehand[193] but may be seen on the Tapestry wielding a mace. This weapon was used by clerics because they were not supposed to draw blood, and hence did not carry swords. Odo has been described as ambitious, greedy and cruel. At one stage he aspired to the Papacy itself, and to that end acquired property in Rome. His tyranny in England in the years after the battle ended with his imprisonment by William until 1087. He finally died in Palermo in 1097.

Ralf de Tosny is also recorded by William of Poitiers as being present.[194] He was half brother of William of Evreux and of a good Norman family, acquiring estates in England.

Roger, son of Turold, may be assumed to have been killed at the battle; this is based on information in the cartulary of Holy Trinity, Rouen.[195] *Robert of Beaumont* is recorded by William of Poitiers as being a young man, and in battle for the first time. He commanded a troop on the right wing and performed and attacked with the utmost bravery and success.[196] He was later created Earl of Leicester.

Robert fitzErneis is said by Robert Wace to have fought and been killed at Hastings, and this is substantiated by a grant he made to Holy Trinity, Rouen, in the same way as Roger, son of Turold, and Gerelmus de Panileuse.

Robert, Count of Mortain, was Odo's brother and Duke William's half brother, and is mentioned by name in the Tapestry. He was involved with Duke William in the initial discussions about the invasion prior to the council of war.

Robert de Vitot is recorded by Ordericus Vitalis as having been present at Hastings, where he received wounds from which he later died. His endowment of certain lands to the monastery of St Evroul, where Ordericus was a monk, would support the accuracy of the record.[197]

It is only in the accepted authority, *Carmen de Hastingae Proelio* by Bishop Guy of Amiens,[198] that any contemporary reference is made to *Taillefer* the minstrel, known as Incisor Ferri.[199] He is recorded as having opened the battle by advancing in front of the Norman army singing traditional songs and juggling with his sword. His undefended position made him an isolated target for the defenders and he was killed.

Turstin, son of Rollo, is recorded by Ordericus Vitalis as having carried the banner of the Norman army at the battle, and on the strength of supporting accounts Professor Douglas accepts Ordericus's accuracy on this point.

Vitalis and *Wardard* are both named on the Tapestry and it has been suggested that the likely reason for this was their personal association with Bishop Odo, who, as designer, would have been in a position to record their names. Both these knights appear in hauberks and mounted on their horses.

Walter Giffard from Longueville-sur-Scie is recorded by William of Poitiers as being present[200] and is specified by Bishop Guy of Amiens as being personally involved in the hacking down of Harold.[201] According to Robert Wace he was quite old, with white hair and a failing arm.[202] He was rewarded with 107 lordships, 48 of them in Buckinghamshire.[203]

William of Poitiers indicates that it was to *William Malet* that the disposal of Harold's body was delegated.[204] He already held lands in Lincoln and Suffolk before the Conquest[205] and by 1069 was Sheriff of York.[206] *William, Count of Evreux*, is also recorded as being present at the battle,[207] he was half brother of Ralf de Tosny and second cousin to Duke William.

William fitzOsbern is referred to by Professor Douglas as the most active inspirer of the expedition after the Duke:[208] he had much to gain from its success. His presence is confirmed by William of Poitiers,[209] and he was made Earl of Hereford in 1067.[210]

William de Warenne, the Duke's second cousin once removed (as his great-aunt the Duchess Gunnor was Duke William's great-grandmother), is recorded by William of Poitiers as having taken part in the battle and later became Earl of Surrey.[211] An unidentified member of the House of Ponthieu is recorded by Bishop Guy of Amiens in his *Carmen de Hastingae Proelio* as having been involved in the killing of Harold. Professor Douglas suggests it could either be *Count Guy of Ponthieu* himself or one of his sons, called *Enguerrand*.[212] As Bishop Guy was

Count Guy's uncle the accuracy of the record is likely to be sound.

The last of the confirmed campaigners is *Humphry de Tilleul en Auge*, who was responsible for the construction of the castle at Hastings, probably on 30 September,[213] and Ordericus Vitalis records that Humphrey commanded the castle from the first day of its construction. He returned to Normandy after the battle to ensure the fidelity of his wife, and forfeited his lands in England.[214]

Of the other five thought by Professor Douglas to have been on the expedition, though not on such strong evidence, *Gerald the Seneschal* was a man of considerable importance at the time, *Hugh d'Ivry* was a member of Duke William's household after the Conquest, *Richard fitzGilbert* was a substantial landowner in England at the time of Domesday, *Rodulf (Ralf) the Chamberlain* was Rudolf de Tancarville, and *Pons* is likely to have been connected with Drogo fitzPons and Walter fitzPons, recorded later as Domesday tenants.

In the front of the Norman army were the archers, who were fast-moving and lightly clothed. They wore close-fitting tunics and knee-length trousers with long stockings, leather shoes, a belt and tight-fitting cap, all designed to facilitate rapid movement and efficient use of the bow. There is one archer illustrated in the Tapestry wearing a full hauberk and helmet; he has removed all the arrows from his quiver and is holding them in his left hand for rapid shooting. This may be a highly trained archer of whom there were only a few.

The standard weapon of the Norman archer was the short four-foot bow, always shown as drawn to the body rather than the ear. There are, however, some longer bows illustrated in the lower margin of the Tapestry. The short bow had an effective range against chain mail of about fifty yards,[215] but was of limited service against leather or wooden shields, in which the arrows stuck and were of no further use. In some cases the archers carried a quiver on their backs or on their hips; in other

Norman archer in hauberk and helmet with empty quiver suspended
from his waist, and arrows held in the left hand. Note the conventionally
dressed archer above with quiver suspended from the shoulder

cases the quivers were larger and stood on the ground. The use
of the four-foot bow is illustrated extensively in the Tapestry,

and there is an isolated example of one being used by a mounted man. He is without armour and may be an archer who grabbed a loose horse at the end of the battle, but he is shooting at the gallop as though an experienced horseman.

It is recorded that the Normans used the crossbow as well,[216] though in what proportion to the four-foot bow it is impossible to say. The crossbow was developed by the Italians in the tenth century and was lethal up to and even beyond 300 yards, though the rate of discharge was slow. It was so deadly that in A.D. 1139 the Lateran Council banned its use against Christians. None is shown in the Tapestry.

The longbow had been in existence since paleolithic times and is known to have been used by the Normans.[217] It is uncertain if any were used at Hastings though some very long staves are shown in the Tapestry. The longbow was not really in military use in Western Europe until the Welsh wars of Edward I 200 years later.[218]

Of William's 3,000 infantry some wore hauberks of chain mail, others leather hauberks and many fought without armour of any sort.[219] The mail hauberks were of the same pattern as those used by the cavalry, that is, a three-quarter-length tunic with loose sleeves to the elbow and the skirt slit front and back. The small circular links of mail were usually closed by rivets and involved lengthy and laborious production. As a result there were never enough in battle – a point well illustrated in the Tapestry, where suits are being removed from the dead during the battle for re-use. The proportion of William's infantry wearing hauberks is difficult to establish and may not have been high.

Hauberks being removed from bodies during the battle for re-use

Of the remainder, many wore thick leather tunics that afforded little protection against sword, lance or axe. Both archers and infantry wore leather shoes constructed from varying thicknesses of leather stitched between upper and sole. The lower leg was criss-crossed with thongs.

The basic infantry weapon of the Normans was the spear[220] with a leaf-shaped head and a slightly heavier wooden shaft than was usual for the cavalry lance. Sometimes a small cross-bar was fitted behind the head so that penetration was not excessive and withdrawal could be rapid. Some of the infantry carried a sword and a few had the great bearded axes of the Vikings more favoured by the Saxons.

The cavalry were by far the best protected and armed section of William's army. They were equipped with the mail hauberk with the short wide sleeves and the skirt split front and back to make sitting on a horse possible; there was a high pommel and cantle at the front and rear of the saddle. Sometimes the hauberk was continued upwards to form a hood or coif to protect the head. There was a slit in the mail at waist level which permitted the sword to be drawn from the scabbard worn underneath. Some of the more important figures in the Tapestry may be seen to be wearing chausses or shin guards, also constructed of ring mail, that were tied at the back of the calf.

In some illustrations of hauberks in the Tapestry there are squares at chest level. Their purpose is uncertain, but they may be some form of attachment for a pad inside designed to take the weight of the heavy suit off the shoulders and eliminate chafing. Clearly these suits, although providing reasonable protection, were extremely heavy, weighing about thirty pounds, and a great encumbrance to free and swift movement. They were usually put on at the last possible moment.

Conical helmets were worn by both infantry and cavalry alike, sometimes over a coif, sometimes without one. These helmets were usually constructed of thin steel hammered to shape and riveted together with radial and circular bands, with the front panel extending downwards to form the nasal.[221]

Helmet with nasal. Note the construction ribs and band at the base of the cone

Sir James Mann further points out that many illustrations in the Tapestry depict the lower rim and the nasal constructed in one piece and riveted to the body of the helmet.[222] There was some variety in the Norman army both in the construction and the quality of the helmets used.

All the cavalry and many of the infantry were equipped with long kite-shaped shields. Sir James Mann interprets the fact that none has survived as indicating that they were made of perishable material such as wood or leather. Their size was approximately 36 inches by 15 inches, although they may have been wider, and it has been suggested that the wooden frame was likely to have been made of limewood.[223] Their shape was most practical as the pointed end protected the vulnerable leg of the rider. They were worn suspended by a loose strap around the neck, and controlled in the left hand by a short strap attached to the inside. The outside or display face was often painted with insignia or symbols.

The main weapons of the cavalry were the lance and the

Norman kite-shaped shield with rim and decoration

Shield straps, illustrating the method of controlling the shield, showing the long shoulder strap and the shorter strap for the hand and wrist

sword. The lance was of the same type as was used by the infantry, with the same leaf-shaped head though without the cross-pieces of the infantry lance.[224] The long shaft was usually more slender and therefore lighter; it was used over-arm above the head, which on horseback would have meant the lance had to be supported in one hand longer than was necessary for the infantryman. Normally the lance was thrown, and if used with a stabbing motion it would have required considerable skill to withdraw it for re-use while remaining mounted.

After discharging his lance, the knight relied on his sword, a much more personal weapon than the expendable lance. It was broad-bladed and little changed from the original Viking sword. The end was slightly rounded with a hollow running down the length of the blade which aided quick withdrawal by reducing suction if a body had been cut through. However, this sword was usually used for cutting rather than thrusting – as shown in the Tapestry. The handle was formed from a metal tang which was a continuation of the blade, protected by a short cross-piece. This metal tang was fitted with wooden grips on each side which were attached by binding.

These swords with their Viking ancestry were very much personal weapons and a great deal of care was taken in their

William, Duke of Normandy, with his mace

manufacture to achieve the right balance and a perfect temper of the blade. The Vikings knew how to convert iron into steel and the Normans inherited this skill, as well as the folding and tempering of iron by water. There was often much superstition and legend attached to a sword.[225]

The other weapon that appears in the Tapestry is the mace. It was used as an insignia of office and sometimes by combatant clergy, who by virtue of their office were precluded from using weapons that were likely to draw blood but could go to war with a blunt instrument.

None of these weapons could be used effectively unless the

Method of saddle attachment using breastband and girth

rider was firm on his horse. The Normans used an elaborate
saddle with a high pommel that was rolled forward in the front,
and an equally high cantle rolled back at the rear. It was held
in position by both breast band and girth, and from it were
suspended the stirrups on leather straps. The Normans rode
very long with a straight leg, as though standing upright. The
horses were all stallions and, with their arched necks and small
heads, look from the Tapestry as though they had Arab blood.
The length of the rider's leg showing below the horse's barrel
suggests that they were small animals, perhaps not more than
fourteen hands.

9

The Saxon Army

Harold's Saxon army may well have been the finest fighting force in Western Europe. It was a superb feat to march about 180 miles in four days to meet the invasion of Harald Hardraade of Norway and to defeat his celebrated army at the Battle of Stamford Bridge.

The Saxon army was made up of two principal parts. The standing regular army consisted of the king's housecarls, a highly trained body developed from the bodyguard of King Cnut about fifty years earlier. This force in normal circumstances was about 3,000 strong;[226] but Hastings was less than three weeks after Stamford Bridge and at Hastings it was unlikely to have been stronger than 2,000. The wounded hardly had time to recover, and there had been another long forced march. These men were supported by the housecarls of Harold's brothers, Leofwin and Gyrth, estimated at about 1,000 men each,[227] which would give a force of some 4,000 regular soldiers. To these should be added an equal number of the Fyrd, and some Danes whom William of Poitiers refers to as 'copious reinforcements'.[228] The Fyrd was a body of part-time soldiers which had been instituted in the reign of King Alfred.[229] They were territorials who were obliged to give two months' service each year and were raised on the basis of one man for every five hides of land, which also raised twenty shillings for his pay and food. Theoretically this could provide a part-time force of between 15,000 and 20,000 men,[230] though there is no possibility that this number of men could have been informed of the crisis, let alone collected together, soon enough to oppose William – particularly as the annual time for service was over. However, Harold could also call on all freemen in times of national emergency[231] such as this, and no doubt he raised what he could in the time available.

The Battle of Stamford Bridge must have had its effect on the Fyrd. Reasonable estimates of the number of fyrdmen who actually got to Harold's standard at Hastings are in the region of 4,000 or just above.[232] This gives a total of a little over 8,000 combatants, much the same as William's numbers. The battle lasted most of the day and was an evenly matched conflict, which suggests evenly balanced numbers.[233]

Harold's army therefore was made up of full-time professional soldiers and part-time fyrdmen, supported by a force of 'Danes' of unknown size (they may actually have been Northumbrians).[234] According to Robert Wace, the men who fought with Harold came from the earldoms of Leofwin and Gyrth, and of Harold himself, plus the places through which Harold marched on his rapid journey south, when he was picking up as many men as he could. The areas listed are: London, Kent, Hertford, Essex, Surrey, St Eadmonds, Suffolk, Norwich, Norfolk, Canterbury, Stamford, Bedford, Huntingdon, Northampton, York, Buckingham, Nottingham, Lindesey, Lincoln, Salisbury, Dorset, Bath, Somerset, Gloucester, Worcester, Hampshire, and Berkshire.[235] This list is consistent with William of Poitiers's reference to a 'vast host' from all the provinces.[236]

The known personalities of the Saxon army are fewer than those of the Norman. There are eleven names of individuals who are known with reasonable certainty to have fought with Harold at Hastings: Leofwin; Gyrth; Aelfwig; Hakon; Leofric; Aelfric; Breme; Godric; Thurkill; Esegar; Eadric. Also cited are 'two freemen of Hampshire' and a 'tenant of the House of St Eadmund'.

Leofwin and *Gyrth* were Harold's brothers. Leofwin, Earl of Kent and Essex, and Gyrth, Earl of East Anglia, were both killed in the battle, their dramatic death being recorded in the Tapestry.

Aelfwig was Harold's uncle and Abbot of Winchester; he died in the battle,[237, 238] but is recorded as having brought twelve monks and a score of soldiers.

Hakon was the son of Harold's brother Sweyn.[239] He had reason for hostility to William as he had been a hostage at William's court since 1052 and was released only after Harold's 'oath' in 1064. His presence made three generations of the Godwine family present at the battle.

Leofric was Abbot of Peterborough and was seriously injured in the battle but managed to return the 150-odd miles to Peterborough to die.[240, 241]

Aelfric of Gelling was killed in the battle; he was a thegn from Huntingdon and a tenant of the church of Ramsey.[242] *Breme* was also killed; he was one of Gyrth's men and a freeman of King Edward's.[243] Two other freemen were also killed; they came from Hampshire,[244] and it may be that these three who were specially recorded as 'freemen' were not members of the Fyrd but able-bodied men called to the defence of the realm.

Godric, who was Sheriff of Fyfield in Berkshire, and held land on lease from Abingdon Abbey, fought and died in the battle.[245] His wife had been in the service of Edward the Confessor, being responsible for his hounds at Abingdon.[246] *Thurkill* also lived in Berkshire and held lands in Kingston Bagpuize as a tenant of Abingdon Abbey; he too was killed at Hastings.[247] Both these Berkshire men are recorded in the chronicles of Abingdon Abbey.

Esegar was Sheriff of Middlesex and may have been in charge of Harold's London contingent.[248] *Eadric* was a deacon from East Anglia and is described as a freeman of Harold.

The armour and weapons of the Saxon army were of diverse quality, partly because of the effect of the Battle of Stamford Bridge, and partly because the army was composed of both housecarls and fyrdmen. Of these the housecarls were the better equipped, and it seems probable that even among them there were two standards of armour – those of Harold's own housecarls and those of the housecarls of Leofwin and Gyrth.

The political and social interchange between England and Normandy before the Conquest was considerable, particularly because of Edward the Confessor's Norman upbringing and early life. The Saxons were familiar with contemporary Norman military development. Indeed Harold himself, having been actively involved in William's border campaigns two years earlier, was fully conversant with the Norman armour and weaponry. So it is quite understandable that the pictorial evidence of the Tapestry suggests that Harold's housecarls, if not those of Leofwin and Gyrth, were equipped with the Norman type of hauberk. It has been suggested that the Tapestry was incorrect on this point,[249] but as it was accurate in displaying some circular shields for the Saxons it was probably correct in the matter of the hauberks as well. The alternative to the hauberk of a leather jerkin with metal rings sewn onto the surface is totally dismissed by Sir James Mann as being weak and ineffective, being no match for a sword stroke and very low on durability.[250]

The scarcity of hauberks is illustrated in the Tapestry by the Norman reclamation of them from the dead during the course of the battle. Their construction was both time-consuming and expensive. This is probably why Harold's housecarls were better provided with armour than the soldiers of Leofwin and Gyrth who are illustrated in the Tapestry with the full Norman type of hauberk, but it cannot be said with certainty how many of their contingents were similarly protected.

While Harold may have lost a third of his housecarls at Stamford Bridge, it is unlikely that the hauberks of the dead would have been discarded and it is possible that all Harold's housecarls at Hastings had hauberks. Also, the booty from Stamford Bridge, largely of weapons and armour, was enormous, and, as already mentioned, was not shared out by Harold contrary to custom.[251] Subsequent supplies should therefore have been plentiful, and Harold's halt in London was long enough for most to have been available at Hastings. Harold's army may have had a more mixed collection of weapons and armour, but this is no suggestion that his housecarls were short of any

Battle Swords. Note that the swords of the opposing sides are of exactly
the same pattern

equipment. So, if an estimate is made of ninety per cent of
Harold's housecarls being protected with hauberks, this gives a
figure of almost 2,500 fully protected housecarls, and Harold
may have had more armoured men than William.

Those of Harold's army who had hauberks probably had the
Norman type of helmet as well, or something very like it. The
conical helmet had been developing in Western Europe since
the fifth and sixth centuries,[252] and was well known to both
Saxon and Norman. The remainder of the Saxon army, made
up of the fyrdmen, wore heavy leather jerkins, trousers, legs
bound with leather thongs, and leather boots. Even though
many of Harold's men rode from Stamford Bridge, a substantial
part of his army must have marched, and their footwear after a
return journey of over 350 miles must have been badly worn.

The Saxon weaponry differed from that of the Normans in
that much more emphasis was placed on the great 'bearded'
axe. This was originally a Viking weapon and could be used to
devastating effect. The blade with its long curved edge of over a
foot in length was slightly asymmetrical and was fitted to the end

A section of the Saxon shield-wall with the archer in front. The small
stature of the archer might indicate that he is a boy

of a handle that was well over three feet long. The axe was of a
high standard of craftsmanship and the blade extremely sharp. It
was an infantry weapon and if correctly swung with two hands,
and sometimes only one, could cause mortal injury to horse and
rider alike.[253] It was particularly effective against cavalry, especially those without lances, as a properly struck horse would
invariably unseat its rider, who in his hauberk was almost
defenceless until he could regain his feet. A Norman rider,
having discharged his lance, must have swung his horse sideways

when he reached the shield-wall, to give him scope to use his sword. This gave the axe-man the chance to bring down his weapon on the horse's unprotected neck. The result is shown in one of the Tapestry's most dramatic scenes.

Many of the housecarls were also equipped with lances of the same type as the Normans. These could be very effectively used by infantrymen against cavalry, particularly when used as a hedge backed by a phalanx of shields against unprotected horses. William of Poitiers refers to axes, spears and javelins being hurled at the Normans and says that even stones fastened to pieces of wood were used, so great was the emergency.

The Saxon housecarls also used swords, again of the same pattern as those of the Normans. With the Saxons, too, the sword was very much a personal weapon, though some of those used at Hastings may have been part of the booty from Stamford Bridge.

They may also have had a small contingent of archers equipped with short bows, though the part they played in the battle was small – only one Saxon archer is illustrated in the Tapestry in front of the shield-wall. It seems likely that many of the Saxon archers did not manage the return march from Stamford Bridge either soon enough or in satisfactory condition to be of any use.

Perhaps Harold's greatest advantage came from his use of the shield, which could be used to good tactical effect by forming a

The round shields used by some Saxon housecarls, possibly those of Harold's brothers Leofwin and Gyrth

close-set defensive wall. Most of his shields were of the same pattern as the long kite-shaped Norman shields with pointed bases. It is possible that as the Saxons did not fight on horseback these shields may have been a little longer than their Norman counterparts. The Saxons also used their own traditional round type of shield, illustrated in the Tapestry, with substantial rims and bosses. These shields are associated in the Tapestry with the death of Leofwin and Gyrth, which suggests that they were used by them and their housecarls. The Tapestry also illustrates an oval-shaped shield, of which there were probably not very many, but a type quite useful as a halfway design between the circular and kite patterns.

10

The Saxon March

After defeating Harald Hardraade of Norway, called by William of Poitiers 'the greatest warrior under heaven',[254] Harold of England's confidence must have been high. It seemed increasingly improbable that William of Normandy would invade during the remainder of the year; and though invade he would, at least Harold had plenty of time to prepare his opposition.

After the Battle of Stamford Bridge the Saxons had the job of clearing up the bodies – of their own dead at any rate – and collecting the booty. How soon after the battle Harold came back to York is not clear, nor is it known when he started south. The days in York must have been spent in resting and in celebrating the victory, caring for the wounded and repairing the equipment. It was on Thursday 28 September – only three days after Stamford Bridge – that William landed at Pevensey, and Wace recorded that a Sussex 'chevalier' who watched the landing rode to York to warn Harold.[255] Bishop Guy of Amiens has Harold being told by a rustic from Hastings, who concentrated more on William's devastation of the countryside.[256] Florence of Worcester states – without giving a date – that Harold was told that William had arrived with a 'countless host of horsemen, slingers and footsoldiers, and help from all parts of Gaul'.[257] General Fuller suggests that Harold received the news on Sunday 1 October,[258] and deduces that as a result of the news he left York the following day and proceeded south at speed. However, the possibility that Harold was already on his way south when the news reached him is suggested by Professor Douglas.[259] This would make the return journey more feasible, even if tradition has it that he received the message while at York. He reached London by Friday 6 October, and he can hardly have had horses for the whole force. It is almost certain that he retraced his steps along what was left, after six centuries of decay, of the Roman Ermine Street through Tadcaster, Ferrybridge and Doncaster to Lincoln and then due south through Peterborough, Godmanchester and Braughing to London.[260]

He was acting now with the same urgency as he had done to meet the invasion of Harald of Norway; Florence of Worcester records that 'Harold did not hesitate to advance with all speed against his enemies'.[261] Knowing his losses at Stamford Bridge, he must have sent messages to his brothers Leofwin and Gyrth to muster all the support they could; though they would probably have heard the news of William's landing themselves, and, being closer to the point of danger, may well have acted on their own initiative.

Harold also sent for help to Earls Edwin and Morcar. They had been decisively defeated at Fulford only a fortnight earlier, but in the light of the new crisis could still be expected to provide some support and follow him to London. He left the government of the northern earldoms in the care of Marlswegen, the Sheriff of Lincoln,[262] but it has been suggested that this might imply some doubts in Harold's mind about the loyalty of Edwin and Morcar.[263]

If Harold received the news while still in York, he achieved almost the same speed on the journey south as he did on the way north. He was marching to defend his own country against a foreigner, the men with him were encouraged by the victory over Harald Hardraade and these factors helped to bring in fresh elements of the Fyrd, for whom Harold sent out messengers in every direction.

Edwin and Morcar, it is recorded by Florence of Worcester,[264] 'withdrew themselves from the conflict'. This implies that they responded to the first call, but then held back – possibly because of their defeat at Fulford and the low morale of their men, but more probably because of their jealousy of Harold. It seems likely that Harold had realised they were not to be relied upon before he reached London.

On the journey probably most of the housecarls would have been mounted, and this vanguard of the army with Harold at its head reached London on 5 or 6 October, the latter being the more likely date.[265] The remainder of the force probably arrived during the following three or four days. There were sections of the Fyrd who followed, composed of thegns with their trained men-at-arms, together with slower infantry and equipment. It is clear, however, that a great many of his men did not arrive in time.

Harold joined forces with Leofwin and Gyrth when he reached London, and the housecarls of the three brothers formed the main strength of the new army. It was probably now that Gyrth tried to dissuade Harold from rushing too quickly into battle against William, and also from continuing in command himself. Ordericus Vitalis emphasises this point, suggesting that Gyrth argued that Harold would perjure himself further by doing so, and that it would be better if Gyrth led the forces against William.[266] Harold rejected this advice, which was supported by his mother, and in the Norman documentation, he is accused of actually kicking his mother when she tried to persuade him to stay with her in London.[267] This is probably part of the Norman attempt to discredit Harold in the eyes of posterity, but might have been sheer frustration at his family's failure to recognise that the 'oath' was made under duress and was therefore invalid.

Harold allowed himself only six days in London. These he used to the full. He must have sent out scouts to discover how much havoc the Normans were wreaking in the area around Hastings and the size and disposition of the Norman force. It is clear that at this stage he was hoping for total victory, as he sent a fleet of seventy ships[268] to guard the South Coast and prevent William's escape by sea.

There were strong arguments for waiting longer in London

before advancing to give William battle. Had Harold been prepared to wait for the rest of his army from Stamford Bridge, and for the thegns from a little further away, he would have had a more substantial army in terms of numbers and allowed his main force, the housecarls, more time to rest. It has been suggested that his impetuosity at this point was the basis of his undoing. However, evidence suggests that he was impetuous only because of the news coming in of the atrocities William was committing in the country around Hastings – Harold's own country.

By now the initial supplies that William had brought with him had run out and the whole of the invading force was living off the country. The longer they had to wait, the further from their base it was necessary for them to go in order to plunder the local populace. This living off the country was a deliberate policy of devastation and terror, not only as a military convenience, but also to frighten the immediate area into submission and to provoke the defence into reacting before they were militarily ready. A psychological battle was taking place between Harold and William before the actual encounter at Hastings. It was William's object to provoke an attack by Harold before the Normans were forced too far from the camp at Hastings and in danger of being cut off from their ships. In this William was altogether successful; by his policy of terror he provoked Harold into rushing to the defence of his realm before his army was fully assembled.

Harold, however, after five days in London, was fully confident that the army he had assembled was sufficient to defeat William. He was not alone in his judgement. William of Poitiers has an account of one Robert, a Norman resident in England and a relative of William, who sent a messenger to the Duke warning him that 'Harold hastens towards you at the head of innumerable troops all well equipped for war. Against them your own warriors will prove of no more account than a pack of curs.'[269]

However, there is no doubt that Harold did leave London

before all the available forces had arrived; Florence of Worcester says that he left in great haste and that he knew 'one half of his army had not yet arrived'.[270] William of Jumièges also states that Harold 'rejected caution'.[271]

William of Poitiers records that a parley took place between the two leaders using monks as emissaries.[272] Harold opened the negotiations by sending a monk to William pointing out that it was Edward's dying wish that Harold should succeed him. After emphasising that deathbed wishes were inviolate, he invited William to return to Normandy with his followers. William then sent a monk, Hughes Maigrot,[273] from Fécamp, to Harold stressing the justice of his own claim and the support of Archbishop Stigand, Earl Leofric, and Earl Siward. In an eloquent plea he further offered to submit his case to either Norman or English law, and to save lives he even offered single combat with Harold. When Harold received this message he replied that he was marching at once to battle. If this is true, and it may be no more than Norman propaganda, then it must have taken place while Harold was still in London, as the reply seems to have preceded the final march.

It is established beyond any reasonable doubt that Harold left London with his main force on Wednesday 11 October.[274, 275] On this march his speed was reduced to about nineteen miles per day by the large number of men without horses.[276] Normally the fully equipped Saxon army of housecarls and some fyrdmen travelled on horses, but on this occasion the support of the unmounted soldiers was deemed essential and even then some were left behind.[277]

It has been suggested that Harold intended to make a night attack[278] or at least to take William by surprise. That he hoped to surprise William seems likely, as this had been such an important factor at Stamford Bridge. The suggestion of a night attack is much more difficult to accept and very much open to question.

After the march of fifty-eight miles across the Weald, Harold assembled his forces within cover of the southern edge of the forest between the villages of Whatlington and Crowhurst, which lie north and south of the Senlac Ridge respectively. Both sides must have sent out scouts as two successive panels of the Tapestry show scouts coming in, first to William and then to Harold, with news of the other's position. Because William's army was camped at Hastings, while Harold's army was making the approach, the advantage of this probably went to William, who would have made sure he knew when Harold left London and would have stationed scouts in the forest. Since Harold was travelling much more slowly on this part of the journey, relays of messengers on horseback could have kept William closely informed of all Harold's movements.

It was probably on the afternoon of Friday 13 October that Harold arrived at the edge of the forest near the assembly point which is referred to in the *Anglo-Saxon Chronicle* as the 'hoary apple tree'.[279] The use of a single significant tree as a landmark was normal at that time,[280] and this would have been a familiar feature to many. Its use by Harold suggests that it stood in open ground but not far from the wooded area that was providing cover for the assembling troops. The approximate position of this tree is now marked by the Caldbec windmill.[281]

Harold also used scouts and one of these is shown in the Tapestry, hiding behind a tree and then reporting William's position to Harold, who is on horseback. William's army was still at Hastings on Friday 13 October, but he would not have moved out so early on the fourteenth – the day of the battle – unless he had news late on the thirteenth of where Harold was assembling on the edge of the forest. Harold's scouts can have had little to report during Friday the thirteenth but must have brought Harold news of the flurry of activity late in the evening, and again when William started to move on the fourteenth.

If Harold had meant to surprise William, it seems unlikely that he envisaged an encounter near the Caldbec assembly point; he may have hoped to achieve his surprise attack by a forced march the next day, perhaps leaving some of his baggage at the end of the forest. Nevertheless his choice of Caldbec as an assembly point was a shrewd one, because in the event of surprise he had his army in the best defensive position the neighbourhood provided.

Harold's men on arrival at Caldbec must have been tired at the end of the day's marching, in spite of the slower rate. The remainder of the force must have been coming in during the night. It would be wrong to suggest that they were exhausted,[282] as only the fittest would have set out from London and these were hardy men, hardened further by their military experience over the past two weeks. However, many of them were short of sleep and were not awake until well after sunrise on the morning of the battle.[283]

Thus the defending army assembled for the encounter with William. It was an army of quality,[284] a fine fighting force depleted only by the losses at Stamford Bridge, and supplemented by the trained men of the Fyrd.

....

The Battle Formations

It is clear from what followed that William's scouts had kept him well informed of the movements of Harold's army, and that he was aware of the approximate number of troops that left London and the speed with which they were travelling towards him. However, he could not have been certain of Harold's assembly point at the Hoary Apple Tree until late in the afternoon of Friday 13 October, too late for a surprise attack, and some of the assembling troops still within the cover of the forest. William's information about numbers must also have been confused by reports of men coming in to join Harold who were still on the march in the forest. At this stage he knew little more than that he had successfully provoked an early encounter.

As darkness fell on 13 October, men were still finding their way through the forest to join Harold, and continued to do so well into the night. These men must have been hungry, and although very fit, tired after their long march. There are Norman stories of English revelries and drinking throughout the night,[285, 286] but these may be dismissed as propaganda.

It cannot be known whether Harold planned at this stage to defend the nearby Senlac Ridge or whether he hoped to attack William nearer Hastings. It has been suggested that Harold may have reconnoitred the Senlac Ridge during his long wait for William in the summer.[287] It is certainly likely that he knew the topography of the locality (the parishes of Crowhurst and What-lington formed part of his personal estates before he became Earl of Wessex)[288] and he chose the Hoary Apple Tree both as a familiar rallying point and as one easily defended in the event of an attack. Perhaps he meant from the start to defend the Senlac Ridge and was waiting for his army to increase in size when he was surprised by William and forced into an earlier conflict than he intended. All he would have needed for almost certain victory was time to erect a satisfactory barricade along the top of the hill, and time for a few more reinforcements to reach him. Some chroniclers say he began to construct defences, but it seems it was too late. Even the weather favoured William; had it rained he would have probably judged the slope too slippery and delayed his attack, thus allowing Harold the valuable time he needed. As it was, by arriving in the early morning of 14 October William achieved partial surprise. Harold had little more time than was necessary to draw up his army as William assembled his force at the bottom of the slope.

The Saxon scouts played an active part in the early hours of 14 October, first telling Harold that the Norman army was on the move, and then bringing details of its further movements until William had passed Blackhorse Hill (TQ 777140). Harold must have been sure of William's intentions by about 8.00 a.m. It is almost certain that by then he had started the deployment of his army along the Senlac Ridge.

Florence of Worcester records that a number of Harold's men deserted.[289] It seems that this report was mere propaganda as he goes on to say that few men remained true to Harold, which is known to be false. In any case it is unlikely that men who had marched from London would have deserted now. If there were any desertions they were minimal.

Harold's men, according to Florence of Worcester, were drawn up in a 'narrow place'[290] which William of Poitiers refers to as 'a position on higher ground on a hill abutting the forest'.[291] This is the Senlac Ridge, which was then likely to have been barren ground.[292] It has been established beyond any reasonable doubt that the Saxon phalanx occupied about 680 yards of the Ridge.[293, 294] It was centred on the site of the high altar of Battle Abbey[295, 296] and ran, at the west end, from a point near the brook west of the Abbey House (TQ 746156) to a point just east of the junction of the Hastings and Sedlescombe roads near the primary school (TQ 754157). This gives a front of a little over 2,000 feet and it would have been made up for the most part of housecarls with possibly a few fyrdmen at the extremities. It is recorded by William of Poitiers that the Saxon line was drawn up 'in very close order',[297] and it has been suggested by Colonel Lemmon that the housecarls stood sideways on. This would give a frontage of about two feet per man or slightly less, which could be protected by a single shield. These shields were not actually linked together[298] though they may in certain cases have overlapped; reducing the frontage per man to less than two feet. This would imply that the front rank of Harold's line was made up of about 1,000 men and behind each were seven or eight more waiting to take their places if required.

It has been suggested that the Saxon line was convex, with the flanks bent back,[299] but it can be seen from the map or on the site that if full advantage was to be gained from the hill the line must have been almost straight. This kept the line on high ground, making frontal attacks on the flanks more difficult for William, and lateral attacks almost impossible because of the natural depressions at each end.[300]

Any suggestion that the Saxon line exceeded this length must be discounted, not only because it would have reduced the density and thus the strength of the line, but more importantly, because it would have exposed the flanks in the lower and more dangerous positions.

Concentrated into less than 700 yards, the Saxon formation presented the finest possible defence against both infantry and cavalry.[301, 302] Forward of Harold's command position the slope down was in the region of 8% (or 1 in 12), reducing to about 4½% on the east flank and 3% on the west. To the rear of Harold's position the slopes were much steeper, being in the region of 15% – too steep to invite attack but not so sheer as to prohibit some sort of retreat should it prove necessary.

In view of the very short time that Harold had to prepare his

The Caldbec Windmill, Harold's assembly point at the edge of the forest, the site of the Hoary Apple Tree

Harold's command position

Aerial view of Harold's position showing Battle Abbey, the primary school (1) and the Caldbec Windmill (2)

William's command post

Aerial view of battlefield

The shallow western slope of the Senlac Ridge

The steeper eastern slope of the Senlac Ridge

The Malfosse gully where many Norman knights perished in their pursuit of the Saxons

The victor – William the Conqueror, from the north face of the north-west tower of Wells Cathedral

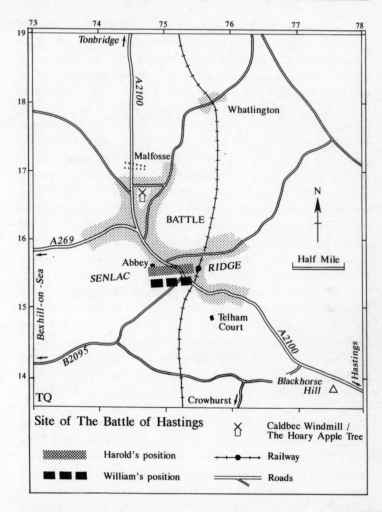

Site of The Battle of Hastings

Harold's position
William's position

Caldbec Windmill /
The Hoary Apple Tree
Railway
Roads

position, it would have been difficult for him to have built any structural defence along this line and none is shown in the Tapestry. At most, a few branches may have been dragged from the forest, but they could have provided only very slight protection.

*

There is evidence from William of Jumièges that while at
Hastings William made preparations against a night attack.[303]
This suggests that he had guessed Harold's intention of repeat-
ing his success against Harald Hardraade by the element of
surprise. To move out against Harold on the fourteenth must
have been a sudden decision, because William had foraging
parties out that had to be hastily recalled.[304] He clearly per-
ceived, when he got the news late on Friday that Harold was
mustering his men at Caldbec Hill, that he had the chance of
turning the tables and achieving some degree of surprise himself.
He knew that the Saxons were still arriving well into the night
and that it was unlikely that they would be considering a battle
early in the morning. William realised that provided he could
gather his army quickly and be forming up at Hastings at first
light,[305] he would catch Harold before he was ready.[306, 307]

This would need preparations and briefing late into the evening and an early start. First light (without the complication of
British Summer Time) would have occurred at about 5.23 a.m.,
an hour before sunrise, depending on the cloud cover, and
William could have been moving his men out by six o'clock.

It is suggested by Robert Wace that the Norman army spent
the night in prayer.[308] This may not mean organised communal
devotion but rather the monks moving among the assembling
troops hearing confessions and possibly giving communion,
while the men prepared themselves for the attack and took
what sleep they could. William, it is recorded, attended Mass
and took communion[309] and this is likely to have taken place
between first light and the departure of the first troops. It may
have been immediately after this Mass, which may have been
celebrated by Bishop Odo of Bayeux, but more likely by
Geoffrey, Bishop of Coutances, that William gave the address
to his troops recorded by William of Poitiers.[310] Details of this
address are not known, nor is it clear who actually heard it –
William could not have been heard by all his 7,000. Perhaps
some leaders were called to the Duke's presence to hear and pass
on his words, or he may have simply spoken to those nearest

him. However, the essence of the message is extremely clear, summarised in a single sentence of William of Poitiers:[311] 'You fight not merely for victory but also for survival.' No doubt the justice of their cause and the Pope's blessing were also stressed. The dangers of losing a battle on foreign soil with the sea behind them must have been apparent to them all. Defeat meant death.[312]

It was at about six o'clock or just a few minutes earlier that the column moved out with the Bretons in the front,[313] probably led by Count Brian of Brittany,[314] though the suggestion has been made that it may have been his brother Alan.[315] Following the Bretons were the Franco-Flemish, almost certainly under the command of Eustace of Boulogne,[316] who may be seen later in the Tapestry restraining their flight before the caption 'HIC FRANCI PUGNANT' ('Here the French fight'). He was assisted by Robert of Beaumont. After the Franco-Flemish came the main Norman contingent under the command of William himself, mounted on a black Spanish charger which was a gift to him from King Alfonso of Aragon when he was returning from a pilgrimage to St James of Galicia.

It has been frequently and erroneously claimed that the Franco-Flemish division was under the command of Roger de Montgomerie but it has now been established beyond reasonable doubt that he remained in Normandy with Matilda at the time of the invasion, and did not arrive in England until December 1067. This is based on a statement by Ordericus Vitalis whose father was a close follower of Roger de Montgomerie and whose evidence in this case Professor Douglas regards as decisive.[317]

The three divisions of William's army each included both cavalry and infantry and must have marched at the best pace the infantry could achieve for approximately five and a half miles to William's assembly point, the highest point of Telham Hill, known as Blackhorse Hill (TQ 777140), on the Hastings to London road. This the vanguard of the Bretons would have reached shortly before half past seven. As Colonel Lemmon points out, little is known of the march discipline, but as it was at infantry pace it is likely that the cavalrymen led their horses with their heavy hauberks laid across their saddles to be donned immediately before the battle. William himself was mounted and must be supposed to have ridden alongside the various sections of the column during the march and to have been at Blackhorse Hill to greet them with encouragement and exhortation and direct them to their battle positions just over a mile further on.

It was probably at Blackhorse Hill, just out of sight of Harold's assembling troops, that the Normans put on their armour[318] and mounted their horses, and then, under the direction of their divisional leaders and guided by the Norman scouts, made their way to the battlefield itself. These scouts are likely to have been in what are now the grounds of Telham Court.[319]

It was also probably at Blackhorse Hill that William donned his armour.[320] It turned to the left[321] as he put it on, presumably resulting in its being back to front, which was seen as a bad omen. He laughed off the incident and did not let the superstition bother him. At some time too, before the battle, he hung round his neck the relics of the saints Ravennus and Rasyphus, the British saints on whose bones Harold had sworn his 'oath' in 1064.[322]

William himself was now ready for battle. Leaving the supply wagons at Blackhorse Hill, he probably followed close behind his own contingent, taking up his command position under the Papal banner and the Leopards of Normandy[323] borne by Turstin,[324] on a slight hill (TQ 753152) in full view of the battlefield and in sight of Harold's phalanx on the top of the opposite ridge. From here he could observe the Bretons moving down the hill and following the brook to take up the left-hand position opposite Harold's right flank. Eustace de Boulogne must have wheeled his Franco-Flemish division to the right on reaching the brook to take up station at the bottom of the slope opposite the Saxons' left flank. Thus the centre was clear to be taken up by the much larger contingent of Normans.[325]

William's army now formed a front about 150 yards from Harold's line, just out of range of the few Saxon archers, and on a contour roughly fifty feet lower,[326] with the steepness of the hill varying from east to west. The Bretons faced boggy ground and heavy going but a shallower slope, while the Franco-Flemish faced firmer ground but a steeper slope. It is recorded that the archers, with arrows and crossbows,[327] were placed in the front, with the infantry behind them and the cavalry at the back. William, although a little behind his formation, was in an extremely good position to supervise the deployment and the first shock of the battle. With him there were likely to have been a small number of headquarters staff, and messengers who could carry detailed instructions to his divisional commanders.

Morale must have been high on both sides. The Normans were on a crusade with Papal sanction, and perhaps the most difficult part of the venture, the Channel crossing, had been successfully completed; while the Saxons had the defeat of Harald Hardraade to their credit and were defending their homeland. The scene was set for one of the most significant events in English history.

The Battle

It needs imagination to capture that moment shortly before nine o'clock on Saturday, 14 October 1066, the Feast of St Calixtus. The two armies were drawn up under a brightening sky with thin cloud cover and no direct threat of rain. Both armies felt the inspiration of unusually gifted and forceful leaders. Harold, aged forty-four, and William, aged thirty-eight, were both in their prime. One mounted, the other on foot, they waited by their battle standards.

William's troops were encouraged by trust in the friends around them and spurred on by the hopes of grants of land. They could be excused, however, some apprehension of these Saxons who had just defeated Harald Hardraade, and whom William of Poitiers describes as 'the fiercest of men'.[328]

As they advanced to their positions they must have fanned out to extend their front,[329] thus thinning their lines in comparison with the densely packed Saxons who looked down at them. The view of the Saxon line about fifty feet higher and some hundred and fifty yards distant must have been forbidding. While it is established beyond reasonable doubt that there was no artificial defence in front of the Saxon line, it is not impossible that they had hammered a few stakes into the ground to protect the end of each flank[330] and it may be these that gave rise to the rumour of a palisade.

What is more important is that William's army may have faced a quagmire. It is possible that the Saxons may, immediately they decided to defend the Ridge, have dammed the Asten brook.[331] This could have caused considerable difficulty

Harold's standard, the Wyvern of Wessex

for the Normans and would have been relatively easy, using logs, brushwood and soil, even though there were less than twenty hours between the arrival of the Saxons and the start of the battle.

From the point of view of the Norman divisional commanders, the attack was going to require all their coordinating ability if they were to exert simultaneous pressure on the Saxon line in spite of the brook and the varying slope of the Ridge from one end to the other. Count Brian had a less experienced division[332] than either the Norman centre under the field control of Bishop Odo and Robert de Mortain, or the Franco-Flemish on the right under Eustace of Boulogne and Robert of Beaumont. Behind the invading army William himself was at his command (TQ 753152), his standard carried probably by Turstin son of Rollo.

From the Ridge, the front row of the Saxons watched the formation below them, confident in their territorial advantage and the strength of their phalanx, which was, William of Poitiers tells us, so tightly packed together that not even the dead could fall.[333] Harold was somewhere near the centre, possibly on slightly higher ground, also with his standards, the Wyvern of Wessex, and his personal banner of the fighting man[334] which may have been based on the Cerne Abbas giant. Clearly he would have been wishing for more time and a storm of rain, as well as reinforcements – none of which he was fortunate enough to enjoy. He knew that victory or defeat lay in the strength of his line. Yet for both leaders this was to be a battle of a new type,[335] with relatively mobile cavalry pitted against static infantry, and this added an element of the unknown.

From a safe vantage point nearby, William's monks and priests watched the deployment of the troops of both sides and anxiously awaited the outcome. The score between Harold and the illegitimate Duke William was about to be settled – Harold, whom William of Poitiers referred to as being 'stained with vice, a cruel murderer, purse proud and puffed up with the profits of pillage, an enemy of all justice and good',[336] and William who later admitted on his deathbed that he had 'wrested the English crown from a perjured King Harold with much effusion of human blood'.[337]

The battle started at about nine o'clock with the slow advance under the Papal banner[338] of William's three divisions, accompanied by the sound of trumpets on both sides.[339] Leading the advancing army was the minstrel Taillefer (Incisor Ferri). Only Guy of Amiens makes any reference to him, recording that he rode before the advancing army singing traditional Viking songs and juggling with his sword until he was cut down by a hail of Saxon missiles. The reliability of this story has been questioned by Brooks and Walker.[340]

As William's archers advanced to within closer range of the Saxon line, spreading out forwards and sideways as they did so, those with static quivers must have stopped and loosed their arrows from one place while others, including some slingers,[341] continued to advance until their ammunition was exhausted. As the archers ran out of arrows, thinned out and withdrew, the infantry started to advance between them. The archery attack almost certainly stopped before William had intended and before the Saxon line was weakened. This was because Harold had very few archers and there were no enemy arrows to pick up and use again. William's archers were shooting uphill, and their arrows were either impaled in the Saxon shields or lost behind the Saxon line, having passed over the enemies' heads.[342]

The Saxons remained in close order awaiting the arrival of the infantry, who must have found it demoralising to climb the fifty feet from the brook to the Saxon line in full armour, only to find that the archery attack had been almost totally ineffective. The first wave of the attack had obviously failed. William of Poitiers refers to the valiant resistance of the English and the death-dealing weight of their projectiles, which included spears, javelins, axes, and stones fastened to pieces of wood. He also records that the Saxon weapons found easy passage through the Norman shields and armour, beating down those who fought at close quarters and wounding those who were shooting from a distance.

William watched all this from his command post. He must have been troubled to see his knights struggling first through the bog, then through the returning archers, before they finally reached the mêlée of armed infantry, in which it would have been difficult for them to have thrown their lances with any degree of accuracy before engaging at close range with their swords. However, they did manage, according to William of Poitiers,[343] to 'rain death and wounds on the Saxons'.

It was probably because of the shallower slope of the hill at the western end that the Bretons reached the top before the other divisions, and, being the least experienced troops, were alarmed by the lack of progress of the other two divisions and the fierce Saxon resistance to the first attack. The Breton cavalry arrived on the Ridge in an uncoordinated attack with their right flank unsupported and found the Saxon shield-wall intact. They were unable to get near enough to the Saxons to inflict damage with their swords without endangering their unarmed horses. Seeing that the charge was weakening and that the Normans and Franco-Flemish were not close enough to be dangerous, the Saxons were able, as best they could in a static formation, to hurl everything they had at the Bretons. At this the Bretons turned and fled back down towards the brook, leaving the approaching

Norman left flank totally unprotected. To this the Saxons could now turn their full attention.

When the Normans and Franco-Flemish finally reached the brow of the Ridge, having also struggled through the hail of Saxon missiles and the mêlée of their own footsoldiers, they too, against all their expectations, ran up against a still solid Saxon shield-wall and, with their left flank exposed, withdrew in considerable disorder. The whole army of the Duke was now in danger of retreat, while the English numbers, according to William of Poitiers, were scarcely diminished.[344]

The fleeing Bretons were pursued, almost certainly against Harold's instructions, by some of the Saxon right wing – again almost certainly not housecarls but the less disciplined men of the Fyrd. They could not see the whole line from their position and may have been under the impression that they had already won and that the whole Norman army was in flight. William's swift response when he saw what was happening was to turn some of the cavalry on the left of the Norman division who had not yet gained the Ridge to attack the pursuing Saxons. William himself must have charged down from his command post, when he saw the opportunity the pursuing Saxons were giving him, to direct his cavalry to cut them down. The pursuing Saxons found the tables suddenly turned and stood at bay on a small hillock near the foot of the slope (TQ 747153). This phase of the battle is clearly shown on the Tapestry. The hillock is now somewhat overgrown but the Tapestry shows only one tree, symbolic of some cover, while the rest of the hillock is clear and depicts Saxon infantry without armour defending themselves against the Norman cavalry. This supports the view that it was fyrdmen who broke ranks, as housecarls would have been wearing hauberks. It is recorded that none of these unprotected men, who were no match for the cavalry,[345] survived the Norman flank attack to regain their line on the Ridge.[346] The Breton retreat was obviously of primary importance. It began as a success for Harold, but soon after turned to his disadvantage. As to when it actually took place, a reasonable estimate would be between 10.00 and 10.30 a.m., which allows an hour for the initial attack by the archers and the subsequent attack by the infantry. It is possible that this attack at the western end of the hill where the slope was shallower may have been cut short by the earlier arrival of the supporting cavalry. It is clear, however, that when they reached the Ridge the Breton cavalry felt unsupported and broke under the concentrated Saxon onslaught. The Tapestry emphasises the hillock on which the pursuing fyrdmen were cut down; perhaps this firmer ground was sought out as a better fighting base because the remainder of the lower ground was marshy or even flooded if the brook had been dammed.

William did not personally take part in the first attack and thus was free to move over and direct the cutting down of the pursuing fyrdmen, and organise the tactical withdrawal of the Norman and Franco-Flemish divisions. These closing stages of the failure of the first attack were critical for William. The Bretons had fled in disorder, the morale of the other two divisions were low and William could easily have failed completely at this point. It has been suggested that had Harold now

The hillock as shown on the Tapestry

charged, victory would have been his,[347, 348] but this seems very doubtful. Infantry with hauberks and axes were ponderous and slow-moving; to pit them against cavalry would have been to throw away all their advantages. The axe was effective against unprotected horses who were attacking a shield-wall, but much less valuable against a rider who had room to circle and manoeuvre, particularly if the infantry in thirty-pound hauberks were fighting in swampy ground. The demoralised state of the withdrawing invaders and their fear of the Saxons were the only factors in Harold's favour had he chosen to risk leaving the Ridge.

The flight of the Bretons and withdrawal of the Norman and Franco-Flemish cleared the brow of the Ridge and immediately took the pressure off the Saxon line, leaving only the debris of battle strewn along the slope. This was the first break or pause in the battle, and it gave both sides a chance to regroup. It would have been impossible to continue all day in hand-to-hand fighting.

Harold, having stuck to his decision to hold his line firm, which was what his survival depended upon, was able to close his ranks and restore his right flank. The dead could be passed to the rear of the phalanx and the more seriously wounded could retire, with help, to seek what care and attention was available from any supporting personnel there may have been behind the line. In front of the line dead horses could be hauled in as barricades, while any dead invaders who had not been removed by their own side would have been left where they lay.

In their withdrawn position at the foot of the slope William was able to reorganise his army back into its three divisions, and separate the infantry from the cavalry. The Tapestry shows hauberks being removed from the dead to be quickly donned by someone else in readiness for the next attack.

The duration of this pause in the fighting need not have been more than between fifteen and thirty minutes. There had been little more than an hour's fighting and there would have been no thought of food. The divisional commanders would have been busy regrouping their sections, issuing more supplies of arrows to their archers, replacing dead or wounded horses and giving detailed instructions, based on the experience of the first attack, as quickly as possible. They would not have wanted to allow the Saxons any more breathing space than they could help.

William's self-possession,[349] his controlled anger at the Bretons' failure and his gift for leadership turned the tide. His army was in imminent danger of defeat but he marshalled them into another concerted attack. In his determination he may have led this second attack personally and after their first failure perhaps nothing but his personal leadership would have brought them again to the assault.

In the light of the Normans' earlier experience, when different divisions arrived at the Saxon line at different times, the second attack must have been much more closely coordinated. The distance between the leading archers and infantry and the following cavalry was probably reduced; the archers would have been by-passed by the armed infantry and cavalry as they discharged their arrows from static positions on arriving within effective range of the Saxons. General Fuller has even suggested that the knights might have been in front in this attack, which probably began between 10.30 a.m. and 11.00 a.m. – based on the probable durations of the initial attack and subsequent pause.[350]

The second assault seems to have been a much more solid and perhaps slower attempt at the Ridge. It was again important for the cavalry to get close enough to damage the shield-wall with their lances, though it is doubtful if they could have done much damage with their swords as long as the wall was intact and their horses unprotected against the Saxon axes. The line was still strong and Florence of Worcester records that the Normans could make little impression.[351] After the first shock of this attack the battle may have developed into a series of smaller, perhaps almost individual battles along the length of what was now not more than 600 yards of frontage.

This second attempt to break the Saxon line may have lasted

Odo, Bishop of Bayeux, encouraging his trainee knights to fight

for up to two hours with one charge after another being thrown back by the strength of the Saxon wall. Large numbers were killed on both sides and as the dead piled up they caused much difficulty to the attacking knights and infantry. William of Poitiers says that many Saxons lost heart at the sight of William[352] but it is questionable whether he could be recognised in his hauberk and helmet. There can be little doubt that by about one o'clock the Saxon line was under heavy pressure that had been sustained for a long time. It was, however, in no danger of breaking; one or two small gaps may have been forced, but they were closed up again from the sides and the rear to prevent the Norman knights actually getting through.

It is clear from the Tapestry that both William and Bishop Odo were active in the fight. Odo may be seen encouraging his trainee knights, who are called 'pueros', 'boys', in the Tapestry. It seems likely that the constant charges against the line were becoming more and more difficult as the slope became more slippery and the obstacles increased.

Eustace of Boulogne, holding the Papal banner, with arms outstretched, stopping the retreat of his Franco-Flemish division

Failure to penetrate the line demoralised the invaders and eventually the Franco-Flemish broke and fled as the Bretons had in the first attack. This William may have foreseen; the Tapestry shows him in the act of restraining the retreat, his helmet thrown back to reveal his face, closely supported by the leader of the Franco-Flemish, Eustace of Boulogne, whose arms are outstretched to stop his fleeing knights while he clutches the Papal banner.

William of Poitiers says there were rumours of William having been killed in the battle.[353] Had these been true the invaders would have probably given up and fled; a mediaeval army was very much the personal following of its leader. It was therefore important that William was seen to be alive and it was for this reason that he threw back his helmet.

This incident has been associated with the Breton rout, but it can be seen from the Tapestry that it forms part of an almost continuous scene in which the adjacent caption is 'HIC FRANCI

William, with his helmet thrown back to reveal his face, stemming the retreat of the Franco-Flemish

PUGNANT' ('Here the French fight'), the clear implication being that these were the same men who had fled and had now returned to the fight. Further, it seems unlikely that William could have been believed dead or wounded after the first attack since he did not actually take part in it but supervised operations from the rear.

It is recorded that William lost three horses during the course of the battle,[354] and at some stages was actually fighting on foot. It was probably the fact that he was not to be seen on a horse that gave rise to the rumour of his death. He cannot have been permitted to remain unmounted for long and Guy of Amiens says that Eustace of Boulogne gave him a horse during the battle.[355] Once remounted he rushed to stop the retreat of the Franco-Flemish, and William of Poitiers records that over the clamour of the battle he shouted a harangue of criticism and encouragement.[356]

Colonel Lemmon has suggested that there were two separate routs of the Franco-Flemish. If this is true, there is no way of telling whether the Tapestry scenes are referring to the first or the second. William of Poitiers also says that the fleeing troops were pursued by some of the Saxons who were again cut down by the wheeling Norman cavalry.

While the Franco-Flemish were in difficulties, the main Norman division was still attacking the Saxon line in the centre, though both sides must have been getting weaker. This struggle probably went on for some time in the form of roughly coordinated charges and individual combats along the front, perhaps until about two o'clock. It has been suggested, too, that it was at this stage that Harold's brothers, Leofwin and Gyrth, were killed.[357] The Tapestry certainly shows them as being killed early in the battle, indeed even before the incident of the hillock, but William of Poitiers refers to their death with that of Harold. The Tapestry is probably not very reliable as to the actual order of events.

William of Poitiers has claimed that William's army twice feigned retreat in order to tempt the Saxons to abandon their strong position and break their shield-wall.[358] This is extremely unlikely as a feigned retreat needs a high degree of discipline in the troops and also control by section commanders; without these it is likely to become a panic-stricken rout. With both cavalry and infantry involved, the need for discipline and training would be even greater, and there is no evidence to suggest that William's army was organised to anything like the necessary pitch for such a manoeuvre. It is still less likely that William would have contemplated a feigned retreat of a part of his force, particularly in the Flemish or Breton divisions which were less under his control – thus leaving the Norman division with its flanks exposed. Certainly the tactic was known at the time,[359] but here the lie of the ground was against it. To have toiled up the slope under an onslaught of missiles only to give up the ground again would have increased the risk of panic and defeat.

The retreats, therefore, were not feigned and are dismissed as

being so both by Sir Frank Stenton and Colonel Lemmon.[360, 361]
The divisions on either wing were generally repulsed and fell
back in disorder. What does seem likely is that William turned
part of the Norman division left or right to combat any Saxons
who broke ranks and came part of the way down the slope. Here
on hard ground the Saxon infantry would have had little chance
of surviving against cavalry, and even less chance of regaining
their position on the Ridge.

It was at this stage of the battle that William withdrew his
whole army to regroup. With parts of it in retreat and parts of
the central cavalry wheeled to counter pursuing Saxons, his
combined attack was in disarray.

The second attack, which formed the central part of the
battle, was the longest phase. It is likely that fighting went on
for perhaps as much as an hour and a half before the retreat of
the Franco-Flemish began. While the repulse of the Bretons in
the first attack probably occurred because the slope of the hill
was less steep on the west side and they arrived at the Saxon wall
before the rest of the army, it may well be that the more severe
slope at the east end caused the repulse of the Franco-Flemish in
the second attack. After a hard struggle to gain the top of the
Ridge and the prolonged encounters each followed by a slight
withdrawal, the Franco-Flemish must have become increasingly
tired and the slope increasingly slippery.

This phase of the Battle must have lasted about an hour
before the weakness of the Franco-Flemish became apparent to
William, who was leading the central attack. He probably then
found it necessary to move across to bolster up Eustace of
Boulogne's command and stem any retreat with some of the
Norman knights. This would have reduced the pressure on the
Saxon centre and prolonged the encounter. The two retreats of
the Franco-Flemish may have been separated by almost two
hours and certainly not less than one, as it would have taken
time to reform them and restore their morale for a further
engagement.

The second phase of the battle therefore probably lasted

altogether for about three hours, taking the time to about two o'clock. At this point, with his men making insufficient impression on the Saxon wall to ensure victory that day, and the Franco-Flemish still in some disarray, William withdrew his army to regroup, rest and re-arm for a last desperate effort.

This second pause in the fighting was an altogether more substantial break than the first one. William, who knew that defeat meant almost certain death, must have wondered as he observed the carnage before him whether he would be able to win the day. Harold, on the other hand, must have been greatly relieved by the respite and encouraged by this second withdrawal of the enemy, though he must have been distressed at his losses. He consolidated his line, filling the gaps, removing the dead and wounded yet again, and passing forward what food and drink was available. The Normans were forced to leave most of their dead near the top of the slope, though there were some whose hauberks could be used again. There were also riderless and frightened horses to be caught.

William now reorganised his three divisions into a single force. Partly because of the reduced numbers[362] and partly because so far the use of three separate divisions had failed, he combined for the final assault the Bretons and Franco-Flemish with his own Norman troops and personally took command.

At this stage in the battle the Saxon wall was still intact, though it must have been a little shorter and perhaps rather thinner than at the start. The Saxons themselves may well have been less exhausted than the Normans as they had not had to struggle up and down the slope, but neither army had had much sleep the night before. The break in action was probably welcome to everyone on the field except William himself, who must have been anxious to finish the battle as soon as possible.

William of Poitiers claims that the Norman numbers were not greatly reduced in the battle,[363] but they had been in action for about five hours and by then William may have lost almost a quarter of his men in dead and wounded, and possibly a slightly greater proportion of his horses, which without armour were so

The turmoil of injured horses

vulnerable to the Saxon axes. With his army in this reduced state and many of his knights fighting on foot,[364] it was imperative for William that the next attack should succeed. From his point of view the outcome of the day now looked precarious. He must have ordered his divisional commanders to bring their troops together so that he could address those within earshot and give instructions to their leaders. His intent was to resume the battle as quickly as possible but he knew he must allow his men as much rest as he could and a chance to get some food and drink.

From his position on the Ridge, Harold, who may now have moved to the front rank,[365] could observe all the Norman movements and make his preparations for their next attack. His shield-wall had held but he too had suffered heavy losses. Survival still depended on holding the line and apart from filling gaps in it and renewing broken weapons, there was little he could do but wait.

It was for William to decide how the next stage of the battle should be fought. He probably discussed with Bishop Odo, Robert de Mortain, Count Brian, Eustace of Boulogne, possibly Robert of Beaumont and others, just how to break the Saxon line. It was clear that the method of sending in the arms of each division separately, with the archers in front, the infantry following, and the cavalry in the rear, had not worked and some other tactic must be applied.

Two factors had caused the previous attacks to fail to break the wall. First, the archers were making no impression by shooting uphill against the shields. The arrows either became impaled or sailed over the Saxon line, while the archers themselves, being unprotected, could not get close enough to do any real damage. Secondly, the horses had no protection against the Saxon axes, which came into play as soon as the riders were close enough to use their swords. Somehow William had to make his archers effective, and enable his knights to get in close to the wall.

It seems likely that in this last attack William placed his archers in the rear, and reduced the depth of his army from front to back. Perhaps he combined cavalry and infantry more closely, interspersing footsoldiers between the knights, his object being to ensure that the whole force arrived at the Ridge together. This was not to be a charge but rather a slow consolidated advance of the whole army, in which no section arrived unsupported. Harold had very few archers, but those he had must have had plenty of Norman arrows collected from behind their lines during the pause in the fighting. It is likely that this Norman advance was made behind the protection of closely held shields, and that the shields stopped any arrows from the Saxon archers.

This last combined assault on the Ridge probably started at about three o'clock under a chorus of abusive banter from the Saxon line as the Normans gradually advanced to within range of the Saxon missiles. If, as seems likely, the plan was to make the advance slow and thus draw as much as possible of the Saxon volley at a longer range, it may have taken as long as half an hour for William's troops to get within hand-to-hand distance of the Saxons.

Just before contact was finally made, William needed to distract the Saxon front line and throw the supporting ranks into confusion. He is known to have ordered the shooting of high-trajectory arrows to fall on the Saxons from above,[366] and this is shown in the Tapestry. It seems likely that this was the moment in the battle when it was done. A shower of arrows launched over the heads of their own men and falling onto the Saxon line would provide just the distraction and confusion the Normans needed to weaken the defence at the moment of attack. This assault was probably the fiercest of the whole day and came in waves of desperate hand-to-hand fighting, perhaps fifteen minutes apart, each supported by high-trajectory arrows.

This may have continued to between half past three and four o'clock, at which point there was a dramatic change in the Saxons' fortune. Weaknesses began to appear in their line and the Norman knights and infantry began to force their way through and split it into sections. This marking the turning

Tapestry detail showing arrows being fired upwards

point in the battle. Up to now the outcome had been in the balance, but once the Saxon defence was breached the Normans immediately held the advantage. The fighting was between men tightly packed together, with unhorsed knights fighting on foot; it was hand-to-hand fighting by men always in danger of being trampled underfoot by injured horses.

For Harold the turn of events was ominous, but his housecarls were still around him and his standard still flew. William, on the other hand, who had been actively involved in fighting on foot[367] with his men in the mêlée of the third assault, could retire once the Saxon line was broken to a position from which he could direct the rest of the battle. He ordered Eustace of Boulogne to lead a combined Norman and Franco-Flemish section in one last offensive against Harold's weakened left flank and they broke through. It is probable that a similar action was successful at the western end of the Ridge and the whole Saxon position was now in great danger.

It may have been at this point that Leofwin and Gyrth, Harold's brothers, were killed. No indication is given in William of Poitiers's account, and the Tapestry is far from clear as to exactly when it happened. In the Tapestry they are shown dying

The deaths of Leofwin and Gyrth

together and as they were leading different troops of their own housecarls, they would hardly at this stage have been fighting side by side. More likely they died at the end of the battle, protecting their king and brother. This is supported by the statement that the three bodies were found together.[368]

It seems likely that the first breach of the Saxon line occurred at about four o'clock and that the battle for the Ridge lasted for about an hour and a half. The first breakthrough must have been followed by increasing confusion, with the battle gradually taking the form of a series of group encounters. There was little Harold could do. If Leofwin and Gyrth were still alive, it must have been now that they fought their way to Harold's side for a final stand. Now it was a matter not of winning the battle, but of life or death.

With his whole army now engaged on the Ridge, there was no reason for William to be directing operations from the rear, and he must have wanted to join in the closing phase of the battle himself. This would mean that for the first time the Norman command was on the Ridge. It is possible that at this stage

Harold's arrest in 1064. He is pictured under the words 'APPREHENDIT'
– not under his name

William may have lost yet another horse under him; this would
substantiate William of Poitiers's claim that the Duke lost three
horses during the battle.[369]

The light began to fade and many of the Fyrd made off into
the forest, where the wounded struggled for cover only to die
when they got there. The groups of housecarls still fighting on
the Ridge grew smaller as man after man fell beneath the
Norman swords. The final fierce encounter around the standard
is portrayed on the Tapestry. It must have been shortly before
half past five that Harold himself was killed, hacked down by a
sword and, in the words of William of Jumièges, 'covered with
deadly wounds'.[370]

The story of Harold being shot in the eye will survive as long as
people talk about Harold and William. It stems from a misin-
terpretation of the Tapestry by Abbot Baudri of Bourgueil[371, 372]
who, about thirty-five years after the Battle, identified Harold as
the figure under the name rather than appreciating that the
captions are normally longer than the scenes to which they refer,

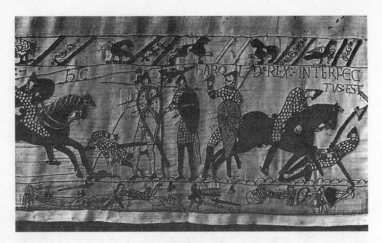

The death of Harold: his figure lies under the words 'INTERFECTUS EST'
(was killed)

and that the figure of Harold is actually under the words 'INTER-
FECTUS EST' (was killed). Comparison of Harold's arrest in 1064
and his death in the Bayeux Tapestry illustrate this point clearly.

Guy of Amiens records that the slayers of Harold were
Eustace of Boulogne, Walter Giffard and Hugh de Montfort,
and one whom he refers to as 'the heir of Ponthieu'. The last
could possibly be Count Guy himself or perhaps his son
Enguerrand.[373] F. H. Baring points out that these four men all
came from the Franco-Flemish division which made the final
assault on the east end of the Ridge.[374] William of Malmesbury
suggests that Ivo of Ponthieu was the fourth person involved and
that it was he who was guilty of the gross mutilation of Harold's
body.[375]

The Norman knights had no doubts about the rightness of
their cause. They were there with Papal sanction to avenge, they
believed, the breaking of an oath by Harold for which he had
been excommunicated and they held those who supported him
to be as guilty of his crime as he was. In their victory they
showed no magnanimity, giving vent to their bitterness at the

loss of so many of their comrades by merciless attacks on dying and wounded Saxons.

After the death of Harold, and without his brothers to lead them, the spirit had gone out of the Saxon defence. Though some groups of housecarls fought doggedly on to the last, others escaped into the forest, only to be pursued by Norman cavalry and cut down if they found nowhere to hide. That a number of Saxons, both housecarls and fyrdmen, fled north during the closing stages of the battle is clear because bands of cavalry of up to fifty men followed in pursuit. They were despatched to prevent the possibility of any regrouping of the Saxons who had escaped. One of these excursions from the battlefield has been well recorded and ended in disaster for the pursuing Norman knights at a place named the Malfosse.

The parishes of Crowhurst and Whatlington were part of Harold's personal estates before he became Earl of Wessex, and he may from his own knowledge have picked the Malfosse for a rearguard action in the event of retreat. It may well have been lined by Saxons before the battle itself actually finished. Much research has been done into the whereabouts of this place, and C. T. Chevallier has established beyond reasonable doubt that the Malfosse is the Oakwood Gill, which runs across the later Battle to London road just a little short of a mile north of the Senlac Ridge (between TQ 744171 and TQ 748170).[376] It is recorded by William of Poitiers that the gully was overgrown, steep-sided and intersected with ditches,[377] and probably difficult to see.

The pursuit towards the Malfosse was led by Eustace of Boulogne[378] to catch a body of men who had fled on seeing Harold killed. This chase by about fifty knights must have started almost immediately after the death of Harold, and no later than half past five because by then the light was fading fast and any cavalry action would have hardly been possible after about a quarter to six. This was probably the largest of the excursions from the battlefield, since it was later followed by William himself. As the purpose was to seek out and destroy fleeing Saxons, the journey of almost a mile over unknown rough ground to the Malfosse may have taken as much as ten minutes.

It is clear from William of Poitiers's account that the Normans were totally unprepared for any organised rearguard action, and were taken completely by surprise as in the gathering twilight they rode headlong into the Malfosse gully. The thick undergrowth that disguised the gully cannot have been very tall or the knights would never have attempted to ride through it. It may have looked like a ha-ha or disguised ditch with a straight drop on the near side and a slope to a higher level on the far side, all lightly overgrown, but in fact quite a formidable gully. The Saxons must have lain in wait behind the bushes near the top on the far side ready to attack the struggling mass of horses and men who had fallen at the ditch. The Normans arrived at exactly the right place for the waiting Saxons and may have been led there deliberately by some of the retreating soldiers.

As he was not injured until afterwards, Eustace of Boulogne seems not to have been in the front of the charge as it reached the gully. He probably pulled up when he saw what had happened, but it was too dark to assess the Saxon strength. He must have realised that there had been heavy losses in the gully and was about to order a retreat when William arrived on the scene. William formed the impression that reinforcements had joined the Saxons,[379] and he ordered Eustace and his men to stand firm.[380] As William was discussing the situation with Eustace of Boulogne, Eustace was struck between the shoulders by a Saxon. The force of the blow was so great that blood flowed from his mouth and nose,[381] and he was carried from the field by his men. William of Poitiers goes on to relate that William himself took charge and in a feat of great bravery, fighting with a broken lance, beat back the Saxons. It does not seem likely, however, that he ventured into the gully.

For Eustace to have been surprised by an attacker he did not see shows that it was dark enough for concealment and probably too dark to differentiate between friend and foe. It is not clear whether Eustace was on horseback or not at the moment of the attack. He may well have dismounted to investigate the situation in the gully. William, on the other hand, having just arrived, was probably mounted. Both men could be immediately identified as Norman because of the horses. The time must have been almost a quarter to six. Many Normans were killed by the Saxons or trampled in the Malfosse gully by falling horses, and among those killed was Engenulf de Laigle.[382]

The incident was too late to affect the main issue. With the final resistance overcome, William and the remainder of the Malfosse force returned to the battlefield. William of Poitiers says that 'he could not gaze without pity on the carnage',[383] though by the time he got back it would have been totally dark and he could only have seen with the aid of lamps and flares. It would have been very difficult to do much more than tend the wounded and feed the hungry. Many, after fighting all day, would have wished for little more than sleep. William pitched his tent and spent the night on the battlefield.

For the Saxons there was no sleep. They fled 'as swiftly as they could, some on horseback, some on foot, some along roads but most over trackless country'.[384] Some were too badly wounded and died where they lay, others were dragged into the forest and left under cover by those who fled. The battle was over.

Harold had died trying to preserve the Saxon way of life that the Saxons loved, he gave his life defending England from the invader and as Professor Freeman put it, 'All that a man could do for his realm and people Harold did'.

13

The Immediate Aftermath

In the morning the 'bloodstained battleground was covered with the flower of the youth and nobility of England'.[385] To picture such carnage as there must have been after a whole day of fighting is difficult. There were probably almost 2,000 Normans and an even greater number of Saxons, a total of about 4,000 men, lying dead along the 600 yards of the Senlac Ridge and the upper part of the slope. These bodies would have been interspersed with between 600 and 700 dead horses, giving at least six human bodies and a horse for every yard of the hill.

It was probably light enough for William and his senior commanders to start identifying friend from foe among the dead soon after six o'clock the following morning, Sunday 15 October. After this identification William himself arranged for the honourable interment of his own men.[386] In view of the numbers involved this was a substantial undertaking for the survivors.

William of Poitiers says that the bodies of Leofwin and Gyrth were found near the body of Harold, though Harold's body had been so mutilated that it could only be identified by certain marks, and then only by his mistress, Edith Swan-neck. William of Malmesbury makes the only reference to Ivo of Ponthieu being dishonourably discharged and sent home by William for cutting off Harold's hands after he was dead,[387] and Guy of Amiens records that the mutilated body was delivered to William wrapped in a purple winding sheet.[388]

Harold's mother, Gytha, offered William her son's weight in gold for Harold's body,[389] but William thought this unseemly and directed William Malet to deal with the burial. William of Poitiers states that it was said in jest that Harold should be buried on the seashore[390] which he had guarded so avidly during the spring and summer; but this William Malet may well have done, bearing the excommunicated body to unconsecrated ground. Tradition has it that it was later moved to Waltham Abbey.

William permitted the bodies of the Saxons to be removed by their relatives rather than have them left to be devoured by wild animals. Senlac Ridge was cleared of fallen soldiers, leaving a mass of broken weapons and many dead horses, and William and his army returned to Hastings.

For William it had been an expensive victory; he is estimated to have sustained losses of about 30%.[391] However, this was the first success of mounted knights against infantry.[392] The Normans had no experience of deploying unarmed horses against axes and the slope had been against them. It was also unusual at that stage in history for a battle to continue for such a long time.

The first attack failed partly because the archery was ineffective and also because the unprotected horses could not press home their uphill attack against the shield-wall. A further weakness was the slightly early and therefore unsupported arrival of the Bretons at the Saxon line.

The second attack failed principally because repeated cavalry attacks made little impression on the wall. They were hampered again by dead men and horses left from the first attack, and by the increasingly slippery nature of the slope. There was also disarray caused by the Franco-Flemish, who broke and fled on two occasions, exposing the Norman right flank. These two retreats, and the withdrawal from the Malfosse that was stopped by William, cast doubts on Eustace of Boulogne's ability and determination.

Had Harold attacked the invaders when they were regrouping at the end of the second phase he might possibly have succeeded. Though the Normans were by then tired and dispirited, it would still have been very risky to pit the Saxon infantry against a combination of cavalry and infantry, and they would have had to fight on marshy ground.

In the last combined attack the flurry of Norman arrows distracted the defenders sufficiently to allow the combined cavalry and infantry to break the line in several places. Once the line had been split into a series of groups and the Norman cavalry were on level ground, the Saxons were no match for them and gradually they were cut down by the invaders.

The sheer length of the battle shows that it was very evenly matched. At that period, when discipline and organisation were primitive, battles were usually over quickly. At Hastings, however, the outcome was still very much in the balance after six hours of fighting, and it cannot be claimed that either leader had out-manoeuvred or out-generalled the other. Certainly there were differences between the two armies but any suggestion that Harold's army was inferior may be confidently dismissed.[393] Its core consisted of the housecarls, who were highly trained professionals. Harold was thoroughly familiar with William's tactics, equipment and horses, but he chose to fight on foot. All his experience had been as an infantry leader and he saw little need to experiment with William's new methods at this crucial time.

Each side had moments of success and failure, of surprise and disadvantage; and it might well be said that luck was the decisive factor.[394] Luck has its runs of good and bad, and for Harold it was bad. He had guarded the coast all summer but the wind kept William away. It was certainly bad luck that he and his army were in the North when William arrived. As it was, the invaders could establish an unopposed bridgehead; it is doubtful if William could have forced his way ashore had his landing been contested.

William's strength lay in his understanding of psychology, both at a political and a personal level. His stage management of Harold's oath and the subsequent conversion of a territorial invasion into a crusade were psychologically brilliant. So, also, was his ruthless devastation of the area around Hastings, designed to tempt Harold into battle before he was ready.

As it turned out, William's decision to bring horses was of paramount importance to his success but only because of the way luck was running. In fact he came within an ace of losing. He won only because he induced Harold into too early a battle and the weather favoured him. Harold lost because he was called to defend his country twice within three weeks, and because he rushed to defend the civilians of Sussex against the carnage, arson and rape of the invaders.

William and Harold fought for the crown of England. Harold was chosen by the Witan and defended his country as a patriot. William made his cause seem just by skilful diplomacy at the Papal court, but his conscience does not seem to have been clear. The words attributed to him on his deathbed by Ordericus Vitalis were: 'I appoint no one my heir to the crown of England, but leave it to the disposal of the eternal Creator, whose I am, and who orders all things. For I did not attain that high honour by hereditary right, but wrested it from the perjured King Harold in a desperate battle, with much effusion of human blood . . .'[395]

He should, on balance, have lost; and apparently the luck that came to his aid at Hastings could not help him win the battle of his conscience.

SOURCE REFERENCES

1 Freeman, E. A., *History of the Norman Conquest of England*, Third Edition, Clarendon, 1877, p. 763.
2 Freeman, E. A., Vol. II, p. 38.
3 *Ibid.*, p. 697.
4 *Ibid.*, pp. 366/7.
5 William of Poitiers, *English Historical Documents*, Vol. 2, 1953, p. 222.
6 *Anglo-Saxon Chronicle*, E. H. D., Vol. 2, 1981, p. 106.
7 Freeman, E. A., Vol. II, p. 452.
8 Stenton, F., *Anglo-Saxon England*, p. 466.
9 Freeman, E. A., Vol. II, p. 456.
10 Freeman, E. A., Vol. II, pp. 429–430.
11 Stenton, F., *Anglo-Saxon England*, p. 561.
12 *Anglo-Saxon Chronicle*, E. H. D., Vol. 2, 1981, p. 118.
13 *Florence of Worcester*, E. H. D., Vol. 2, 1981, p. 218.
14 *Anglo-Saxon Chronicle*, E. H. D., Vol. 2, 1981, p. 122.
15 *Ibid.*, p. 120.
16 *Ibid.*, p. 123.
17 Stenton, F., *op. cit.*, p. 566.
18 Douglas, D. C., *English Historical Review*, Vol. LXVIII, 1953, p. 528.
19 Douglas, D. C., *op. cit.*, p. 545.
20 *Anglo-Saxon Chronicle*, E. H. D., Vol. 2, 1981, p. 124.
21 Florence of Worcester, E. H. D., Vol. 2, 1981, p. 220.
22 *Anglo-Saxon Chronicle*, E. H. D., Vol. 2, 1981, p. 126.
23 Florence of Worcester, E. H. D., Vol. 2, 1981, p. 220.
24 *Anglo-Saxon Chronicle*, E. H. D., Vol. 2, 1981, p. 125.
25 Freeman, E. A., *op. cit.*, pp. 334/5.
26 Florence of Worcester, E. H. D., Vol. 2, 1981, p. 221.
27 Thierry, A., *A History of the Conquest of England by the Normans*, Dent, 1901, Everyman, p. 142.
28 Stenton, F., *op. cit.*, p. 568.
29 *Anglo-Saxon Chronicle*, E. H. D., Vol. 2, 1981, p. 222.
30 *Ibid.*, p. 130.
31 William of Poitiers, E. H. D., 1953, p. 217.

32 William of Jumièges, E. H. D., 1981, p. 228.
33 Gransden, A., *Historical Writing in England*, c. 550–1307, Routledge & Kegan Paul, 1974, pp. 103–104.
34 Thierry, A., *op. cit.*, p. 138.
35 Martimort, A. G., '*The Eucharist*', Irish University Press, 1973, p. 214.
36 Thierry, A., *op. cit.*, p. 140.
37 Stenton, F., '*The Bayeux Tapestry*', Phaidon, 1957, p. 167.
38 Thierry, A., *op. cit.*, p. 139.
39 Freeman, E. A., *op. cit.*, Vol. III, p. 245.
40 William of Jumièges, E. H. D., 1981, p. 229.
41 Matthew, D. J. A., *The Norman Conquest 1066*, p. 77.
42 Freeman, E. A., *op. cit.*, Vol. II, pp. 553–4.
43 Stenton, F., *op. cit.*, p. 577.
44 Freeman, E. A., *op. cit.*, Vol. III, p. 22.
45 *Anglo-Saxon Chronicle*, E. H. D., 1981, pp. 137/8.
46 Freeman, E. A., *op. cit.*, p. 305.
47 Thierry, A., *op. cit.*, p. 143.
48 Florence of Worcester, E. H. D., 1981, p. 225.
49 Freeman, E. A., *op. cit.*, p. 692.
50 Florence of Worcester, E. H. D., 1981, p. 225.
51 Hassall, W. O., '*Who's Who in History*', Blackwell, 1964, p. 52.
52 Freeman, E. A., *op. cit.*, p. 581.
53 Freeman, E. A., *op. cit.*, pp. 44–45.
54 Matthew, D. J. A., *op. cit.*, p. 74.
55 Freeman, E. A., *op. cit.*, p. 580.
56 William of Jumièges, E. H. D., 1981, p. 229.
57 *Anglo-Saxon Chronicle*, Vol. II, 1981, E. H. D., p. 143.
58 Matthew, D. J. A., *op. cit.*, p. 76.
59 *Cambridge Mediaeval History*, Vol. V, C. U. P., 1926, p. 482.
60 *Ordericus Vitalis*, E. H. D., 1953, pp. 166/7.
61 Hassall, W. O., *op. cit.*, p. 50.
62 Furneaux, R., *Conquest 1066*, Secker & Warburg, 1966, p. 66.
63 *Ibid.*, p. 66.
64 Florence of Worcester, E. H. D., Vol. II, 1981, pp. 225–6.
65 *Anglo-Saxon Chronicle*, E. H. D., Vol. II, 1981, p. 144.
66 Freeman, E. A., *op. cit.*, p. 64.
67 Freeman, E. A., *op. cit.*, p. 68.
68 Stenton, F., *op. cit.*, p. 581.
69 *Ibid.*, p. 582.
70 Freeman, E. A., *op. cit.*, p. 182.
71 *Anglo-Saxon Chronicle*, E. H. D., Vol. II, 1981, p. 144.
72 Florence of Worcester, E. H. D., Vol. II, 1981, p. 226.
73 *Anglo-Saxon Chronicle*, E. H. D., Vol. II, 1981, p. 144.
74 William of Poitiers, E. H. D., Vol. II, 1953, p. 220.
75 Freeman, E. A., *op. cit.*, p. 390.

76   William of Poitiers, E. H. D., Vol. II, 1953, p. 220.
77   Furneaux, R., *op. cit.*, p. 55.
78   *Anglo-Saxon Chronicle*, E. H. D., Vol. II, 1981, p. 144.
79   Florence of Worcester, E. H. D., Vol. II, 1981, p. 226.
80   *Anglo-Saxon Chronicle*, E. H. D., Vol. II, 1981, p. 144.
81   Stenton, F., *op. cit.*, p. 587.
82   *Ibid.*, p. 587.
83   Florence of Worcester, E. H. D., Vol. II, 1981, p. 226.
84   *Ibid.*, p. 226.
85   *Ibid.*, p. 226.
86   William of Poitiers, E. H. D., Vol. II, 1981, p. 229.
87   Freeman, E. A., *op. cit.*, p. 339.
88   *Anglo-Saxon Chronicle.*, E. H. D., Vol. II, 1981, p. 146.
89   Furneaux, R., *op. cit.*, p. 56.
90   *Anglo-Saxon Chronicle*, E. H. D., Vol. II, 1981, p. 145.
91   Florence of Worcester, E. H. D., Vol. II, 1981, p. 226.
92   Matthew, D. J. A., *op. cit.*, p. 80.
93   Freeman, E. A., *op. cit.*, p. 336.
94   Furneaux, R., *op. cit.*, p. 86.
95   Florence of Worcester, E. H. D., Vol. II, 1981, p. 226.
96   Brooks, F. W., *The Battle of Stamford Bridge*, East Yorks Historical Soc.,
     1956, p. 11.
97   *Ibid.*, p. 12.
98   Matthew, D. J. A., *op. cit.*, p. 16.
99   Brooks, F. W., *op. cit.*, p. 12.
100 *Anglo-Saxon Chronicle*, E. H. D., Vol. II, 1981, pp. 148/9.
101 Brooks, F. W., *op. cit.*, p. 13.
102 *Anglo-Saxon Chronicle*, E. H. D., Vol. II, 1981, p. 148.
103 Magnusson, M., *Vikings*, BBC London, 1980, p. 310.
104 Furneaux, R., *op. cit.*, p. 94.
105 *Anglo-Saxon Chronicle*, E. H. D., Vol. II, 1981, p. 148.
106 Brooks, F. W., *op. cit.*, p. 14.
107 Brooks, F. W., *op. cit.*, p. 21.
108 William of Poitiers, E. H. D., Vol. II, 1953, p. 222.
109 Florence of Worcester, E. H. D., Vol. II, 1981, p. 227.
110 *Anglo-Saxon Chronicle*, E. H. D., Vol. II, 1981, p. 146.
111 Grierson, P., *Relations Between England and Flanders Before the Conquest*, Trans.
     Royal Hist. Soc., No. 23, 1941, p. 110.
112 *Ibid.*, p. 110.
113 *Anglo-Saxon Chronicle*, E. H. D., Vol. II, 1981, p. 146.
114 Freeman, E. A., *op. cit.*, p. 374.
115 Furneaux, R., *op. cit.*, p. 102.
116 Brooks, F. W., *op. cit.*, p. 16.
117 Douglas, D. C., *William the Conqueror*, Eyre & Spottiswoode, 1964, p. 399.
118 Magnusson, M., *op. cit.*, p. 311.

119 Florence of Worcester, E. H. D., Vol. II, 1981, p. 213.
120 Freeman, E. A., Vol. III, p. 43.
121 Loyn, H. R., *The Norman Conquest*, Hutchinson, 1971, pp. 33–4.
122 William of Poitiers, *English Historical Documents*, Vol. 2, 1953, p. 218.
123 *Cambridge Mediaeval History*, Vol. 5, 1926, p. 497.
124 Fuller, J. F. C., *The Decisive Battles of the Western World*, Eyre & Spottiswoode, 1954, p. 369.
125 William of Malmesbury, *De Gestis Regum Anglorum*, Vol. 2, Eyre & Spottiswoode, 1889, p. 299.
126 William of Poitiers, *op. cit.*, pp. 218–19.
127 Thierry, *op. cit.*, p. 151.
128 *Cambridge Mediaeval History*, *op. cit.*, p. 489.
129 William of Poitiers, *op. cit.*, p. 219.
130 Freeman, E. A., *History of the Norman Conquest of England*, 1869, p. 320.
131 Fuller, *op. cit.*, p. 367.
132 Hassall, W. O., *Who's Who in History*, Blackwell, 1964, p. 52.
133 Thierry, *op. cit.*, p. 148.
134 William of Poitiers, *op. cit.*, p. 219.
135 *Ibid.*, pp. 219–20.
136 *Cambridge Mediaeval History*, *op. cit.*, p. 498.
137 Fuller, *op. cit.*, p. 372.
138 Archibald, E. H. H., *The Fighting Wooden Ship in the Royal Navy*, Blandford, 1972, p. 1.
139 *Ibid.*
140 Brooks, *op. cit.*, p. 10.
141 Magnusson, M., *The Vikings*, BBC, 1980, p. 40.
142 Archibald, *op. cit.*, p. 2.
143 Freeman, *op. cit.*, p. 379.
144 *Cambridge Mediaeval History*, *op. cit.*, p. 499.
145 Douglas, D. C., *William the Conqueror*, Eyre & Spottiswoode, 1963, p. 398.
146 *Ibid.*, p. 396.
147 Loyn, *op. cit.*, p. 44.
148 *Cambridge Mediaeval History*, *op. cit.*, p. 499.
149 Douglas, *op. cit.*, p. 203.
150 Thierry, *op. cit.*, p. 154.
151 William of Poitiers, *op. cit.*, p. 221.
152 *Ibid.*
153 Douglas, *op. cit.*, p. 398.
154 William of Jumièges, *English Historical Documents*, Vol. 2, 1953, p. 216.
155 Freeman, *op. cit.*, p. 384.
156 *Ibid.*, p. 399.
157 William of Poitiers, *op. cit.*, p. 221.
158 Lemmon, C. H., *et al.*, *The Norman Conquest*, Eyre & Spottiswoode, 1966, p. 90.
159 Ashley, M., *William the Conqueror*, Weidenfeld & Nicolson, 1973, p. 38.

160 Freeman, *op. cit.*, p. 410.
161 William of Malmesbury, *op. cit.*, p. 300.
162 William of Jumièges, *op. cit.*, p. 216.
163 William of Poitiers, *op. cit.*, p. 222.
164 Thierry, *op. cit.*, p. 159.
165 *Ibid.*
166 *Cambridge Mediaeval History, op. cit.*, p. 497.
167 Douglas, *op. cit.*, p. 196.
168 Freeman, *op. cit.*, p. 408.
169 William of Jumièges, *op. cit.*, p. 216.
170 Mason, J. F. A., *English Historical Review*, 1956, p. 64.
171 Freeman, *op. cit.*, p. 733.
172 Douglas, *op. cit.*, p. 64.
173 Fuller, *op. cit.*, p. 372.
174 *Ibid.*
175 *Ibid.*, p. 371.
176 *Cambridge Mediaeval History, op. cit.*, p. 498.
177 *Ibid.*
178 *Ibid.*, pp. 488–9.
179 *Ibid.*, p. 372.
180 Douglas, D. C., 'The Companions of the Conqueror', *History*, September 1943, pp. 129 ff.
181 Mason, *op. cit.*, pp. 61 ff.
182 Douglas, *op. cit. (History)*, p. 139.
183 William of Poitiers, *op. cit.*, p. 229.
184 *Ibid.*, p. 225.
185 Douglas, *op. cit. (History)*, p. 141.
186 *Ibid.*, pp. 139–40.
187 *Ibid.*, p. 137.
188 William of Poitiers, *op. cit.*, p. 227.
189 Douglas, *op. cit. (History)*, p. 139.
190 Douglas, *op. cit.*, p. 203.
191 Maclagan, E., *The Bayeux Tapestry*, Penguin, 1943, p. 26.
192 William of Poitiers, *op. cit.*, p. 225.
193 *Ibid.*, p. 227.
194 Loyn, *op. cit.*, p. 34.
195 Douglas, *op. cit. (History)*, p. 141.
196 William of Poitiers, *op. cit.*, p. 227.
197 Douglas, *op. cit. (History)*, p. 140.
198 *Ibid.*, p. 138.
199 Gransden, *op. cit.*, p. 98.
200 William of Poitiers, *op. cit.*, p. 227.
201 Douglas, *op. cit. (History)*, p. 139.
202 William of Poitiers, *op. cit.*, p. 229.
203 Pine, L. G., *They Came with the Conqueror*, Evans, 1966, p. 80.

204 William of Poitiers, *op. cit.*, p. 229.
205 Pine, *op. cit.*, p. 13.
206 Douglas, *op. cit. (History)*, p. 138.
207 William of Poitiers, *op. cit.*, p. 227.
208 Douglas, *op. cit. (History)*, p. 134.
209 William of Poitiers, *op. cit.*, p. 227.
210 Douglas, *op. cit. (History)*, p. 134.
211 William of Poitiers, *op. cit.*, p. 227.
212 Douglas, *op. cit. (History)*, p. 139.
213 Mason, *op. cit.*, pp. 61 ff.
214 *Ibid.*
215 Loyd, A., *The Year of the Conqueror*, Longmans, 1966, p. 212.
216 William of Poitiers, *op. cit.*, p. 225.
217 Blackmore, H. L., *Hunting Weapons*, Barrie & Jenkins, 1971, p. 144.
218 Wilkinson, F., *Edged Weapons*, Guinness Signatures, 1970, pp. 115–16.
219 Wilson, G., 'Norman Arms and Armour', *England under the Normans*, British History Illustrated, 1978, p. 8.
220 *Ibid.*, p. 10.
221 Mann, J., 'Arms and Armour' in Stenton, *op. cit.*, pp. 58–9.
222 *Ibid.*
223 Lemmon, *op. cit.*, p. 92.
224 Mann, *op. cit.*, p. 67.
225 *Ibid.*, pp. 65–6.
226 Tetlow, E., *The Enigma of Hastings*, Peter Owen, 1974, p. 158.
227 *Ibid.*, p. 159.
228 William of Poitiers, *op. cit.*, p. 225.
229 Lemmon, *op. cit.*, p. 92.
230 Tetlow, *op. cit.*, p. 159.
231 Loyn, *op. cit.*, p. 115.
232 Tetlow, *op. cit.*, p. 159.
233 Lemmon, *op. cit.*, p. 101.
234 Freeman, *op. cit.*, p. 747.
235 *Ibid.*, p. 423.
236 William of Poitiers, *op. cit.*, p. 225.
237 Tetlow, *op. cit.*, p. 146.
238 Freeman, *op. cit.*, p. 426.
239 Douglas, *op. cit.*, Table 7.
240 Tetlow, *op. cit.*, p. 146.
241 Freeman, *op. cit.*, p. 426.
242 *Ibid.*, p. 425.
243 *Ibid.*
244 *Ibid.*, p. 730.
245 *Ibid.*, p. 425.
246 Tetlow, *op. cit.*, p. 147.
247 *Ibid.*

248 Freeman, *op. cit.*, pp. 729–30.

249 Lemmon, *op. cit.*, p. 98.

250 Mann, *op. cit.*, p. 62.

251 Brooks, *op. cit.*, p. 16.

252 Mann, *op. cit.*, p. 59.

253 Freeman, *op. cit.*, p. 47.

254 William of Poitiers, *op. cit.*, p. 222.

255 Stenton, Frank, *William the Conqueror*, Putnam, 1925, pp. 190–1.

256 *Ibid.*

257 Florence of Worcester, *op. cit.*, p. 213.

258 Fuller, *op. cit.*, p. 373.

259 Douglas, *op. cit.*, p. 399.

260 Margary, I. D., *Roman Roads of Britain (South East)*, Phoenix, 1955.

261 Florence of Worcester, *op. cit.*, p. 213.

262 Stenton, *op. cit.* (1925), p. 192.

263 *Ibid.*, p. 193.

264 Florence of Worcester, *op. cit.*, p. 214.

265 Douglas, *op. cit.*, p. 399.

266 Ordericus Vitalis, *The Ecclesiastical History of England and Normandy*, trans.
     T. Forester, Bohn, 1853, p. 482.

267 *Ibid.*

268 *Ibid.* p. 483.

269 William of Poitiers, *op. cit.*, p. 222.

270 Florence of Worcester, *op. cit.*, p. 213.

271 William of Jumièges, *op. cit.*, p. 216.

272 William of Poitiers, *op. cit.*, pp. 223–4.

273 Thierry, *op. cit.*, p. 161.

274 Douglas, *op. cit.*, p. 399.

275 Fuller, *op. cit.*, p. 373.

276 *Ibid.*, p. 374.

277 *Ibid.*

278 Ordericus Vitalis, *op. cit.*, pp. 482–3.

279 *Anglo-Saxon Chronicle*, *op. cit.*, p. 144.

280 Tetlow, *op. cit.*, p. 151.

281 *Ibid.*, plate 11.

282 Douglas, *op. cit.*, p. 197.

283 *Ibid.*, p. 198.

284 Fuller, *op. cit.*, p. 373.

285 *Ibid.*, p. 374.

286 William of Malmesbury, *op. cit.*, p. 302.

287 Lemmon, *op. cit.*, p. 100.

288 *Cambridge Mediaeval History*, *op. cit.*, p. 500.

289 Florence of Worcester, *op. cit.*, p. 214.

290 *Ibid.*

291 William of Poitiers, *op. cit.*, p. 225.

292 Douglas, *op. cit.*, p. 199*n.*

293 Fuller, *op. cit.*, p. 376.

294 Douglas, *op. cit.*, p. 199.

295 *Ibid.*

296 Fuller, *op. cit.*, p. 376.

297 William of Poitiers, *op. cit.*, p. 225.

298 Lemmon, *op. cit.*, p. 101.

299 Stenton, *op. cit.* (1925), p. 196.

300 Fuller, *op. cit.*, p. 376.

301 Stenton, *op. cit.* (1925), p. 195.

302 Fuller, *op. cit.*, p. 376.

303 William of Jumièges, *op. cit.*, p. 216.

304 *Ibid.*, p. 224.

305 *Ibid.*, p. 216.

306 Douglas, *op. cit.*, p. 217.

307 *Anglo-Saxon Chronicle, op. cit.*, p. 144.

308 Fuller, *op. cit.*, p. 374.

309 William of Poitiers, *op. cit.*, p. 225.

310 *Ibid.*

311 *Ibid.*

312 Loyn, *op. cit.*, p. 94.

313 Lemmon, *op. cit.*, p. 104.

314 Douglas, *op. cit.*, p. 199.

315 Stenton, *op. cit.* (1925) p. 198.

316 Fuller, *op. cit.*, p. 377.

317 Douglas, *op. cit. (History)*, p. 144.

318 Lemmon, *op. cit.*, p. 103.

319 Tetlow, *op. cit.*, p. 163.

320 Baring, F. H., *Domesday Tables*, St Catherine, 1909, p. 226.

321 William of Poitiers, *op. cit.*, p. 225.

322 *Ibid.*

323 Lemmon, *op. cit.*, p. 103.

324 Ordericus Vitalis, *op. cit.*, p. 483.

325 Lemmon, *op. cit.*, pp. 103–4.

326 *Ibid.*

327 William of Poitiers, *op. cit.*, p. 225.

328 William of Poitiers, *op. cit.*, p. 228.

329 Fuller, *op. cit.*, p. 378.

330 Baring, *op. cit.*, p. 222.

331 *Ibid.*, p. 132.

332 Tetlow, *op. cit.*, p. 177.

333 William of Poitiers, *op. cit.*, p. 226.

334 Brooks, N. P., and Walker, H. E., *Proceedings of the Battle Conference 1978*, Boydell Press, 1979, p. 32.

335 William of Poitiers, *op. cit.*, p. 227.

336 *Ibid.*, p. 222.
337 Ordericus Vitalis, *op. cit.*, p. 311.
338 William of Poitiers, *op. cit.*, p. 225.
339 *Ibid.*
340 *Proceedings of the Battle Conference 1979*, Boydell Press, 1980, p. 4.
341 Florence of Worcester, *op. cit.*, p. 213.
342 Douglas, *op. cit.*, p. 199.
343 William of Poitiers, *op. cit.*, pp. 225–6.
344 *Ibid.*, p. 226.
345 Douglas, *op. cit.*, p. 200.
346 William of Poitiers, *op. cit.*, p. 226.
347 Fuller, *op. cit.*, p. 379.
348 Douglas, *op. cit.*, p. 199.
349 Stenton, *op. cit.* (1925), p. 220.
350 Fuller, *op. cit.*, p. 379.
351 Florence of Worcester, *op. cit.*, p. 214.
352 William of Poitiers, *op. cit.*, p. 228.
353 *Ibid.*, p. 226.
354 *Ibid.*, p. 228.
355 Freeman, *op. cit.*, p. 748.
356 William of Poitiers, *op. cit.*, p. 226.
357 Freeman, *op. cit.*, pp. 485–6.
358 William of Poitiers, *op. cit.*, p. 227.
359 Douglas, *op. cit.*, p. 201.
360 Stenton, *op. cit.* (1925), p. 198.
361 Lemmon, *op. cit.*, p. 109.
362 *Ibid.*, p. 110.
363 William of Poitiers, *op. cit.*, p. 228.
364 Lemmon, *op. cit.*, p. 110.
365 William of Jumièges, *op. cit.*, p. 216.
366 Lemmon, *op. cit.*, p. 110.
367 William of Poitiers, *op. cit.*, p. 228.
368 *Ibid.*, p. 229.
369 William of Poitiers, *op. cit.*, p. 228.
370 William of Jumièges, *op. cit.*, p. 216.
371 *Proceedings of the Battle Conference 1978*, p. 25.
372 Gibbs-Smith, C. H., 'The Death of Harold at the Battle of Hastings', *History Today*, March 1966, pp. 188–91.
373 Douglas, D. C., *op. cit. (History)*, p. 139.
374 Baring, *op. cit.*, p. 229.
375 Tetlow, *op. cit.*, p. 181.
376 Chevallier, C. T., 'Where Was Malfosse?', *Sussex Archaeological Collections*, Vol. 101, 1963.
377 William of Poitiers, *op. cit.*, pp. 228–9.
378 Fuller, *op. cit.*, p. 381.

379 William of Poitiers, *op. cit.*, p. 228.
380 Ordericus Vitalis, *op. cit.*, p. 483.
381 William of Poitiers, *op. cit.*, p. 229.
382 Ordericus Vitalis, *op. cit.*, p. 486.
383 William of Poitiers, *op. cit.*, p. 228.
384 *Ibid.*
385 *Ibid.*, p. 229.
386 *Ibid.*
387 Tetlow, *op. cit.*, p. 181.
388 Ordericus Vitalis, *op. cit.*, p. 487.
389 William of Poitiers, *op. cit.*, p. 229.
390 *Ibid.*
391 Lemmon, *op. cit.*, p. 115.
392 Douglas, *op. cit.*, p. 19.
393 Loyn, *op. cit.*, p. 97.
394 *Ibid.*
395 Ordericus Vitalis, *op. cit.*, p. 311.

INDEX